# CHANGE
# THE FUTURE:
# FORGIVE

"I beg you,
please forgive the trespasses of your brothers
and their sin;
for they did evil to you"
(Genesis 50:17 NKJV).

Forgiveness is the bridge between our history,
our hurts and our future.

# PETER BURNETT

Change the Future: *Forgive*

# DEDICATION

To the descendants of African slaves.

# ACKNOWLEDGEMENTS

It was my late grandparents, Mr. Amos Waite and Mrs. Keturah Waite, who, by their lives and words, first taught me the principles of forgiveness. So, it is with respect and gratitude that I think first of them

This book is also about my mother, Rev. Patricia Waite. She practiced forgiveness every single day of my life. She reminds me to be a voice, and never an echo.

I also want to acknowledge my former and present colleagues, instructors, and mentors as well as those who receive our ministry in Jamaica, the Caribbean, USA and beyond. Thank you for your contribution to our journey in life and ministry.

I also thank those who pushed me to discover the value and power of forgiveness. The testing gave me this testimony.

Our children: Phillip, Elizabeth, Christopher and Christine, are our joy and delight. They walk with us on this journey. Thank you for your unconditional love and the many times you supported your mom and I do God's will. The Lord keeps the book. Your mother and I love you.

Last, but not least, I thank my sweet and beautiful wife, Betty. You have been a steady encourager, and the love of my life. Thanks for your prayers and unwavering support. I thank God for joining us together for His Glory.

# Table of Contents

**Introduction:**

Rev. Dr. Martin Luther King Jr. called forgiveness the central pillar of healing and real harmony among people. In this book we are presented with clear evidences that the time has come to put the focus on forgiveness. It is time to choose forgiveness as the united response to all wrongs committed during the sad dark days of slavery, and for the discrimination and prejudice that followed and continue even to today.

While many books have been written on the continuing revolution in civil and equal rights globally, most of the emphasis has been on the responsibility of the offending individuals, system or society. We have demanded reformation from others, and rightly so. However, the time has come for the final stage of that revolution. The focus and responsibility most now shift to us, the victims of discriminations and descendants of slaves.

I call it Phase II. The central principle is forgiveness. It is the final hurdle to bring harmony in the land and a sense of "settledness" or healing to those who have been hurt, discriminated against or injured. Un-forgiveness is the big elephant in the room that no one wants to talk about. I believe that this is the missing message that our young people are waiting to hear. Why is it that in spite of the monumental achievements by people of African descent across the Western Hemisphere, there is still an underlying feeling of anxiety, un-appreciation, unsettledness and disconnection?

Who is responsibility to forge deeper levels of harmony and true unity among people brought together in our nation by two very different sets of circumstances? Is the responsibility only that of those in the majority race? Is it all about politics, reparation, redistribution of wealth and "getting my piece of the pie"? What can we do? I believe that it is time to shine the light on this subject. Isn't it time for individuals to find their own voice about their past

6

and the kind of future which they desire for themselves and their children, and not just echo the conclusion of others.

I draw upon my own Jamaican heritage and my wife American-African heritage as well as study to communicate these important life changing principles. A brief review of the influential perspectives that continue to shape the debate among people of African descent is also provided. This is also a practical guide on how to actually forgive others, regardless of the nature of the offense.

Readers will appreciate the invitation to finality and settlement to an argument that seems to have no end. They will leave with a clear understanding that harmony among people from very different backgrounds is truly within reach, but it is not automatic and cannot be legislated. In fact, in this book I show why I believe that much of the external or political stage is already in place for personal success and to remove the shame of slavery from our faces. We have nothing to be ashamed of.

The major hurdles of today are not external. They are internal. The dark clouds of unforgiveness overshadows and mask the future. To live in unforgivesness is to blow up the bridge to the future. Unforgiveness makes true progress, proper relationships and peace impossible to find. This book will enable the reader to deal with the issues that are delaying, blocking or stealing their success.

This is also a universal message. Everyone will benefit by reading it, because the principle of forgiveness can be applied to people from Afghanistan to California and Cape Town to Zimbabwe.

# Chapter 1

## It's Time for change.

"When the music changes, so must the dance."
(Nigerian proverb).

The social landscape is changing around us. The real issue is whether we are willing to acknowledge those changes. Things are quite different today than they were in the 1950s or 60s. There are few similarities between the society in which our fore parents lived and ours today, especially when compared to our ancestors who suffered the injustice of slavery. We can't even compare our experience with theirs. In fact, I would have to say that society is far more advance, inclusive and global today than I expected it to be. More people are deliberately communicating, interacting and intermingling outside their communities and ethnic groups than ever before.

The discussions on race relations rarely focus on building on the positive. Much of the improvement in race relations in the last few decades have been taking place below the radar. In a January 2010 article to honor Rev. Dr. Martin Luther King Jr., columnist Juan Williams stated that the agreement on shared values across racial lines is about to eclipse the history of slavery, legal segregation and suspicion. He pointed to poll results from the Pew Research Center for the People and the Press which found that 70 percent of white Americans and 60 percent of black Americans believe that values held by blacks and whites were merging.

People of African descent in the USA, in the Caribbean, and across the western hemisphere are being called upon to acknowledge and embrace change in this new millennium. We are facing the challenge of dancing to a new tune. How should we deal with all these changes? How should our thinking change about those linked to the great pain and hurts of the past?

Our perception of ourselves and our social standing is also being challenged by this new reality. Racial and cultural lines have already been breached. Globalization is no longer a theory. It is a reality. The world is getting smaller. Mixed and cross-cultural marriages are increasing.

The interaction between races and cultures will only intensify. What will you do when someone from the race which oppressed you or your fore parents calls you family? This pressure is causing us to confront our painful past. We will have to do more than just get along. We will have to do better than burying the issue. The time is right for healing. Harmony is the by-product of healing.

Forgiveness enables healing. It is the only way to deal with those who offend you or those whom you dislike, fear, distrust or compete against. Forgiveness is an approach to life that leads to a higher dimension of living. It opens up a quality of freedom which is deeper and more secure than any legislative action. Forgiveness also places your focus upward and fills your hearts with peace, destiny, new dreams and joy.

Come with me on this journey. I'm definitely a work in progress, however I hope to show you that there are many people who have scaled the hurdles of a painful past and are living beyond the prison of their history. This is not a "pie in the sky" approach. In fact, I believe that forgiveness is the only realistic, honest and proper approach to those who have trespassed against you.

My own journey began in a little town called Yallahs in St. Thomas, Jamaica. It's still the best place to get a juicy East Indian mango or to find the national tree of Jamaica, the rock solid lignum vitae. My journey included both physical and mental change. However, the journey to destiny, and healing does not require a physical relocation, only a willingness to change ones thinking and learn from experience.

As a student at Morant Bay High School I enjoyed participating in the Jamaica Combined Cadet Corp, and I looked forward to a possible career in the Jamaica Defense Force. However, when I graduated from High School I was just too young to follow up on my plans. I pick up a brief census job at the Statistical Institute in Kingston.

A few years earlier a team of students from Christ For the Nations Institute in Dallas, Texas had visited Yallahs on a summer mission trip. I had a miraculous life changing experience during their visit, and so after they returned to Dallas they petitioned the leadership of the CFNI to extend a work scholarship to me to attend the Bible College. I also needed a special exemption due to my age to attend the school. I received the exemption and was granted a work scholarship to attend Christ For the Nations Institute, a Bible College in Dallas, Texas in January 1983. I was only 16 years old. My mother sold her only cow to buy my airplane ticket for Bible College in the USA.

That experience forever marked my life. I am forever grateful to those who believed that God had a bigger plan for my life than I could see. I've learned that it takes family, friends, and even strangers to help us to grasp the big picture of life. I've learned that fears, past hurts, hidden agenda, vendettas and prejudice can undercut opportunities and close open doors.

My journey out of my comfort zone challenged me to learn to deal with new things, new people, new relationships, new insults, new hurts and new opportunities. There were no guarantee of success, and there never is, just opportunities. Every leg of the journey was critical, because I was my mother's only child. We had no idea where the journey would end up, except she said, and I agreed, that God held my future and not man. Faith in God is critical to finding healing from the hurts in life, and experiencing peace and harmony in life.

I returned to Jamaica in 1985 determine to put in practice the things I learned in Bible College. I still remember my friends at home asking me about my car, clothes and the American dollars which they expected me bring back home. At times I felt like a failure, because I had nothing to show for the path I had chosen.

My journey has taken me a long way since then. Today I have been blessed with a wonderful wife and four young adult godly children. My family is a multi-cultural affair. We are a blend between Jamaican and African American roots. My wife was born in Belle Glade, Florida, but grew up in a little town in upstate New York called Geneva. My children were born in Montego Bay, Jamaica and Gillette, Wyoming. I've had the privilege of ministering in many different nations and in many different cultural settings. We have had the opportunity to build very meaningful and valuable cross-cultural relationships with many friends over many years now. Has it been without suffering hurts, slights and insults? No, but such is the journey of life.

One of the great joys in my life was being a part of the pioneer team of Caribbean Christ For the Nations Bible and Vocational Institute in Reading, St. James, Jamaica in 1987. This was an extension of the very Bible College which I attended in Dallas, Texas. The vision was to help other "nobodies" like myself to learn what I had discovered. CCFNI helped many men and women from across the Caribbean capture a bigger picture of life outside their communities. It is a great blessing, many years after the closing of that school, to meet former students from Jamaica, Trinidad and Tobago, Haiti and other Caribbean nations as well as from the USA and beyond, who are at peace with the truth that God held their future and not man.

In 1999 my family and I moved to Florida and began attending New Harvest Church, in the small sugar town of Clewiston, on the banks of the Okeechobee River. This book started when Bishop Tony Miller, the pastor at that time, preached a message from Jeremiah chapter 29 and verse 11. The verse says, *"I know the plans that I have towards you says the Lord. Plans of good and not of evil. To give you a future and a hope."*

This particular verse is probably one of the most frequently quoted verses in the Bible. I would often quote it to the Bible College students to encourage them to get God's big picture for their lives. However, that Sunday morning the message stirred something deep within me which I could not contain. I was broken and the tears flowed uncontrollably. Betty, my wife, asked me if I was okay. I said, "yes" only because I knew how to be okay. However, my tears were, and continue to be, for my children, and the many people - children, youth and adults - of African roots across the USA, the Caribbean and the western hemisphere. I was weeping because many of them were still saddled with the pain of rejection, discrimination and unsettled history. Many assumed that the powerful or the well-connected had hidden plans which controlled their future.

I still weep for those isolated, and unsettledness because of the loss of their family history and ethnic heritage. I weep for those who have been brainwashed into seeing themselves through the eyes of others. I weep for those who see themselves as victims. I weep today for all those who have no idea that there is a way to be "okay." Many have concluded that there is no God, no plan, no future, no change and no hope.

Today after more than three decades of ministry, I have no regrets. I can boldly say that attending Bible College and challenging my comfort zone was the right decision. I have had the opportunity to meet people from all over the world. I've learned a few things along the way. One of the most important lesson is that people are people. Sometimes you have to step outside the community to experience a new life, create new ways of living and learn new things. The times are changing and changing fast. Now is the time to widen the pool of knowledge and reach out to help others to find the path beyond the past.

Who would have thought that a man of African descent would be the President of the United States of America? Yet on November 4, 2008, Mr. Barack Hussain Obama was elected as the

44<sup>th</sup> President by popular vote. Four years later he defied all odds again to become one of the few two-term Presidents in the history of the United States of America. Conventional wisdom said that he did not stand a chance. Many pundits and "wiser heads" did not believe that a majority of the population would actually vote for him, not with a strange name, a black skin and to top it off, an African father and white mother. However, all the rules were broken.

The world is no longer what the wise guys told us that it was. We're beyond the old lines. A paradigm shift has taken place. And we will never go back to the way it was, no matter who occupies the White House.

The story of former First Lady Michelle Obama is also an indication of the dramatic changes which have taken place around us. Researchers were able to positively identify her great-great-great-grandparent. The news media reported:

> In 1850, the elderly master of a South Carolina estate took pen in hand and painstakingly divided up his possessions. Among the spinning wheels, scythes, tablecloths and cattle that he bequeathed to his far-flung heirs was a 6-year-old slave girl valued soon afterward at $475. In his will, she is described simply as the 'negro girl Melvinia.' After his death, she was torn away from the people and places she knew and shipped to Georgia. While she was still a teenager, a white man would father her first-born son under circumstances lost in the passage of nearly two centuries.

> In the annals of American slavery, this painful story would be utterly unremarkable, save for one reason: This union, consummated some two years before the Civil War, marked the origins of a family line that would extend from rural Georgia, to Birmingham, Ala., to Chicago and, finally, to the White House.

There's, no doubt, universal agreement that the former First Lady Michelle Obama is worth a lot more than the US $475 valuation placed on 6 year old Melvinia Shields. In fact, it is immoral to even conjure up a "dollar value" for any human being, including the wife of the former President of the United States of America. This is the 21$^{st}$ century. Things are much different from 1850, and even the 1960s. I understand though that the hurt remains, because many of us are unable to identify our roots. We just don't know their names. It leaves us to feel disconnected to society, but that is just one response. Another equally powerful response could be to accept the mess as our history and build a new life. For example, to be Caribbean has its own social, cultural and linguistic uniqueness.

I understand that the pain and offense is so deep and personal that to go beyond it seems like a sellout. It seems disrespectful, and impossible. But hold on, you're in good company. Do you believe your ancestor would rather your chained to the hurts of slavery instead of crossing over the bridge of forgiveness into your future? It is hard to truly appreciate the gigantic changes in our world today unless you give yourself permission to break away from thinking like everybody else. It's the old story of not being able to see the forest because of the trees.

I'm inviting you to come outside the community for a while. It means daring to explore a different perspective. It means being open to new ways of looking at old problems. It is daring to believe that the answers to your most vexing questions are within your reach.

There is a story in the Bible where Samaria was surrounded by the mighty King Ben Hadad of Syria (1 Kings 6). The water supply was cut off and the economy was destroyed. The top selling food items in the market were donkey's heads and doves' dung! It was a full-blown economic, political, spiritual and social siege.

The King of Israel was completely overwhelmed. He, and his advisors, embraced the popular perception that God either caused or allowed the problems; consequently there was no use to trust in God for the solutions. Religion was sidelined and deemed irrelevant. They had a completely negative perception of the problem. They could see no path to victory, especially after throwing out the "God option." And that is not unusual. Forgiveness cannot be experienced without embracing the "God option." The "God option" was central to scaling the hurdles to achieve the abolition of slavery, the emancipation declaration, the civil rights, etc, etc. So don't throw away the map before the journey is over. The "God option" must make a comeback in order for us to find harmony.

I'm sure that the leaders of that day held many conferences on the history and reputation of the Syrian army. They had every right to itemize the injustices and list the wrongs. In fact, they probably held court every day to rehearse the horror of their experiences. They expressed their feelings like we do; with works of art, movies, stories and songs. I wonder how much of their creative energy was spent worrying. You cannot be worrying and creative at the same time. This approach is no different from those who continue to see the invisible hand of others, "the man", and "the society", "the system or Babylon" in the destruction of our community. Parents are still telling their children and young people that they have to represent the entire black race and out work everybody else, because they won't get a fair shake because they are black. That is a lot of pressure to put on the shoulders of children and young people. It's not working.

A new movement is rising. While the King of Israel was scratching his head and the media was just retelling the same "breaking news" over and over again, there was a prophet named Elisha who had a different perspective. There are Elisha-like voices among us today, and they will not be silent. For the "Elisha kind of people", the "God option" is never off the table. They

15

believe that God has a solution for the crisis we face. They believe that there is a better way to motivate our children and young people to work hard and do their best.

Elisha told the King and his advisors that in a 24 hour period the entire siege would be over and the economic problems and death sentence over the community would be lifted. Needless to say, they laughed at him. In fact, one of the high officials openly insulted both God and Elisha. He mocked Elisha, He announced that if God could work miracles, it could happen, but since God can't, it won't. They assumed that their position gave them the full rights to all wisdom. Today, the wisdom of the Church is still underrated in spite of her success in advancing human dignity, education, social justice, and other major issues in life.

Thankfully the preacher was not deterred. Thankfully the Rev. Dr. Martin Luther King was undeterred by naysayers. Elisha prophesied that the official would see the changes with his own eye but would be unable to participate or benefit in it. The official would not cross the bridge into the future.

Well, sure enough the changes took place. The "informed people" didn't even know that the dynamics on the ground had shifted. Unbeknown to them the Syrian army had melted away into the night. Their strongholds were broken, and their control was over. The monopoly of the Syrian Army, those mighty oppressors who erected barriers to power, wealth and success was forever destroyed. In reality, the threat no longer existed, but the King, the media, and the "informed advisors" continued to believe that they did.

We need to measure the change by visiting the street corners not more seminars and conferences. There were four un-named lepers sitting at the gate of the city during the siege of Samaria. They were the outcast from their community, because of heir contagious condition. At some point these four outcasts stirred up enough courage to do something about their terrible predicament.

16

They got sick and tired of generational cycles. They decided to take the risk and venture outside the walls of their community.

If what you are doing is not working then what is wrong with trying something different? You will need to develop the courage to ask the tough questions about your situation, before you will be able to change it. These questions might cause you to do the unthinkable. It could lead you to experience the unbelievable. The four men who took the risk were all lepers. They were in a worse condition than the entire city. Their family and community could not be of help to them. They had a record. Their reputation and livelihood were gone. They clung to each other like a bunch of bad peas in a pod. They had nothing to lose. They said, *Why are we sitting here until we die? If we say, 'We will enter the city,' the famine is in the city, and we shall die there. And if we sit here, we die also. Now therefore, come, let us surrender to the army of the Syrians. If they keep us alive, we shall live; and if they kill us, we shall only die."* We have a saying in Jamaica that goes like this: "betta mus com." The lepers were committed to "beta".

These lepers experienced a paradigm shift. This kind of shift happens when someone is willing to ask the questions, take the risk and make the decisions to change the norm. A paradigm shift happens when it is no longer rational to maintain the present way of doing things, and a clear justification for change is embraced. We do not know the names of these condemned men, but their bravery changed many lives. They moved forward and discovered to their surprise that the Syrians were gone. The problem was nonexistent.

I submit to you that in the 21$^{st}$ century you won't have to fear the same things which confronted your parents, grandparents and forefathers. Many of the problem which overwhelmed them no longer exist. The decision of four lepers shattered the false perception that was literally choking the life and progress out of the majority of the people.

What did these lepers have over the people in the city? They decided to confront their fears. The result was that they were able to experience the blessings of freedom and increase. Note that the skin color of the lepers remained the same, but their future was changed. Meanwhile, the "informed people" like the King, his advisors and the majority of the community believed that the siege existed, when it had ended. The political leaders were still defining a future based on the old problem. They were still paying big money for a donkey's head and dove's dung.

Perception creates experience, but your experience might not be reality. The status quo changed when the rest of the city was willing to listen to four lepers. At first they were suspicious. Who believes the word of an outcast? Many times unless you have access, education, the right family background, some influence and popularity your message might linger in the dust for a while, but only for a while. Truth will always prevail, because only reality is reality. Real change will come to our cities and communities and nations when the old school thinking is rejected by the people.

Old ways of looking at the world, and at others will have to be thrown out to get the blessing of life in the 21$^{st}$ century. People of African descent will have to reach deep and make forgiveness the next order of business. Parents will have to teach about this new perspective. Forgiveness must be added into the narrative of our story. Worldviews that were formed during times of oppressions must no longer be tolerated, because this is a new season. Old worldviews forged in the heat of battle, conflict and resistance to oppression must be deliberately identified, given the appropriate and honorable place in history as we move forward into the future.

I sincerely believe that there will be an explosion of joy, creativity, innovation, growth, prosperity and development when people in our villages, cities, suburbs and towns all across America, the Caribbean and the Western Hemisphere embrace this new reality. Things that government official and the "talented third" have dreamed of getting done, will suddenly happen.

Those of us whose ancestors were once slaves and servants are being healed and ushered into our destiny. There will be a time when a majority of the African Diaspora will believe in the principle of forgiveness, and firmly place the past in its rightful place. I believe that time is now. It's time for a new paradigm.

# Chapter 2

## A Paradigm Shift

The root meaning of the word "paradigm" is an example, a pattern or to show alongside. It's like a model. My grandmother, the late Keturah Waite, used patterns to make the clothes for her ten girls, for her grandchildren, a host of other relatives and friends. I still remember her pedaling away late into the night on that old brown Singer sewing machine with her head wrapped and her eyeglasses propped on the tip of her nose. The smoky kerosene lamp was her only light. Its yellowish glow would cast a larger than life picture of her on the wall of our little wooden house. She would lean forward ever so slightly as she daintily moved the cloth under the needle; carefully following the newspaper pattern she had previously cut. We also follow patterns and models in our thinking and reasoning process.

In a community there are patterns, norms and expectations. Certain outcomes are expected, almost predetermined. I've been told, "If you lie with dogs, you will get fleas." That was the expected outcome before someone invented a chemical to get rid of dog fleas! The evil of slavery, subjugation, racial discrimination and the not-too-distant legalization, political sanctioning and major profiteering from these activities, makes it is perfectly understandable that the perspective of people of African heritage is different on this issue than those of non-African descent. Our view is, and should be, affected by our personal connection to the story.

Our perception of history affects our worldview. Our life experiences and the stories we hear all play a major role on the way we see life and on our expectation out of life. Your perception can make you indifferent, bitter or better. Many social scientists believe that by age 13 our worldviews are already formed, and that by early adulthood they are reinforced or redefined by experiences, and are then transferred to the next generation in our adulthood.

Worldview is transferred by stories, life styles examples, as well as our songs, movies, arts, and through education.

The days of the "us" vs them" are over, but that is no good unless you believe that those days are really over, and you are willing to give yourselves, and each other, the freedom to act like its over! Our worldview must line up with the fact that those days are over. Am I saying that everyone is well meaning today? Is discrimination or prejudices erased from the earth? Of course not, that is an unrealistic expectation. It is common knowledge that even among brothers and sisters of the same race, certain words and descriptions are used when we want to inflict the most pain. We know which phrases will sting, and sting very deep, when we really want to hurt someone. Those kinds of attitudes can only be changed on the personal level. However, enough evidences of change exist on all fronts to make holding on to outdated worldviews inexcusable.

There are no longer any laws in the United States, the Caribbean or western hemisphere which sanctions or supports slavery, subjugation and the entrapment of people. The ending of the African slave trade in the Western hemisphere had the ripple effect of ending slavery globally. And even if there is more work to be done, the framework is in place. The laws are definitely on the books. And I would argue that positive action from people of African heritage on the forgiveness front is what is needed now.

Although slavery was bad, wicked and wrong, we must appreciate the fact that the lives and suffering of our fore parents were not in vain. Most vivid is the fact that the old practices of slavery and subjugation have been forever exposed as morally bankrupt, wicked and bad. The United Nations Human Rights Charter declared this evil method as illegal even for prisoners of war.

Before the Atlantic Triangle collapsed and the abolition movements gained momentum in Europe and later in the Americas, the State Churches supported slavery, superiority and the subjugation of one group by another. Selected portions of the Bible were used to assuage the consciences of men and women, and prop up false doctrines, but not anymore. It was not long after the reformation of the 1400s and the availability of the Bible to ordinary people that those old mindsets began fall. People began to see clearly that the God of the Bible was not a supporter of slavery, racism, subjugation, prejudice, discrimination nor isolation of people. A proper reading of the Bible exposed the consciences of the people to the truth. We live with the result of that paradigm shift today.

Across the world there is widespread religious and spiritual clarity on the issue of slavery. In fact, any religious or spiritual movement that discriminates, or is racists, or intolerant of others is universally stained and suspected. We need to remember that this was not always the case. We have come a long way. Today, even though not all religions or religious groups have completely rejected the practice or the belief of superiority based on color, ethnicity or lineage, we have made significant progress. In fact, in some circles there is reverse discrimination taking place, because those who were once discriminated against have the power to now turn the tables on those who caused the pain. Sometimes bad behavior seems to be transferred easier and quicker than the common cold! Two wrongs never make a right. False doctrine is only removed by the bold teaching of the truth.

Darwin's Theory of Evolution existed as a philosophy many years before he articulated it. It has been the dominant worldview of secular and non-Christian societies for centuries. This philosophy teach that men were unequal; some were born as kings, some as rulers, merchants, and servants or even as gods. They believed that some people were naturally inferior and had the physical make up for hard labor and outside work, while others were the thinkers and rulers. This worldview believes that the process of natural selection determines the destiny of the individual. This philosophy made it easy to accept as norm the practice of slavery, subjugation, superiority and discrimination, as well as the "soft-bigotry of low expectation." And so for centuries depending on where you were born, your ethnicity could then work for you or against you.

Hitler took the theory of evolution to its ultimate conclusion. He became the selector. The general view is that those who accept the evolutionary theory today do not follow it to this extreme. Although the fact that abortions are promoted so heavily in the African-American, Caribbean and other non-European communities is a cause for concern. We should remain on guard to preserve and expand the freedoms we have.

We must not be ashamed of our ancestors, and we dare not downplay their amazing accomplishments. When we deny the progress that we have made, we belittle the awesomeness of their journey. What other group of people have made such progress? We need to revisit the reasons for the progress. How is it that we have come so far? It is important to answer that question in case we are tempted to believe that one person can turn back the hand of time.

Our hurts and fears can be manipulated by smooth operators. They work on our fear of reliving the past for their own benefit. There are many sweet-talkers ready to use your bad experiences to their advantage. People can use your fears to keep you off balance and gain an advantage over you. Your fear can be your worst enemy.

There is no way that slavery; Jim Crows laws, segregation and race-based policies will dominate our lives again. I am not delusional. My head is definitely not in the sands. I'm just stating the truth. We have simply crossed over those lines. We should not be afraid to say so. That gene is out of the bottle.

If we travel the highways in the US, it won't be long before we crossover various state lines. To refuse to acknowledge the existence of the new state does not erase it. Many years we flew into Florida to preach a circuit that ran from Florida to Dallas to

Wyoming and back. We would load up our four kids, and they would fall asleep as soon as we hit the road.

Although everything looked the same at the borders between each state, we knew we had driven across the line because the mile markers would decrease and then start to increase all over again. We had to pay attention to the signs along the road. The States had "welcome signs" lit up like a Christmas tree at all hours of the night. We were the same persons on both side of the state line. The geography was the same, but we had definitely crossed over into another state. The descendants of African slaves have crossed over many lines and borders. We need to acknowledge them, accept them and begin to have a conversation about our expectation of life on this side of the victories. We need to change our perception to match the new reality. We need leaders to focus on life on this side of our journey.

Numerous global, national, federal and state laws have been enacted to ensure that the system is no longer set up to favor "the man" or any one group. The Voting Rights Acts of 1965 makes it possible for the people to hold each politician accountable and to allow them to have a say in the laws and rules that impact them at the local level. There is an office in the US Federal Government called the Office of Civil Rights. They monitor and hold states accountable for the enforcement and vigilance on this issue. This group is themselves accountable to the President and to the US Congress.

Today, Justice Clarence Thomas, a descendant of African slaves, is an influential member of the Supreme Court of the Unites States. Other descendants of African slaves like retired General Colin Powell once led the most powerful military force the earth has ever seen. Others are multi-billionaires today. Many own and lead successful businesses that reach across the globe. They lead the largest Christians denominations of today. Churches led by leaders of African heritage across the western hemisphere are just too numerous to list and they continue to grow daily. Leaders of

24

African descent continue to sway enormous influence and power across the globe.

Today, people of African descent are well educated. They are preachers, professors, college presidents, politicians, doctors, teachers, students, inventors, trade men, etc. We have so much success and progress that it is to the point now where it is becoming unnecessary to celebrate every new field in which people of African descent are excelling. Above all the capacity exists for us to become educated, and to learn whatever we choose to.

We have definitely crossed the line socially. The number of mixed marriages is increasing daily, not yearly. Laws prohibiting mixed marriages are archaic and unheard of in these days. It would take a complete destruction of the United States of America for that kind of segregation to take place again. The schools are integrated. Health care is integrated. The restaurants are integrated. The Civil Rights laws are now entrenched in American political life.

The roots of the Civil Rights laws are now even connected to many other issues that have nothing to do with race. These laws simply will not be uprooted without tearing at the very moral fabric of the land. Numerous advocacy groups, lobby groups and watchdog groups exist to protect these rights. It is no longer a dream. It is a reality. I've met many who participated in the civil right marches, and I want to hold them and say, "The dream came through. We're here now. What happens next?" We have crossed some significant milestones. These advances should inform our perception of the future.

People of African heritage can now use their vast and influential political power to affect entire nations. Political parties realize that individuals are now free to vote the way they want to. The herd mentality is over. Group thinking is over. The community vote is over. A key principle of the new paradigm is that the responsibility is now on aspiring leaders to earn the support they get. The days of automatic party line or support along racial lines should be over. Leader should not be elected because of their skin, familiarity nor history, but because of their ideas. Vision is the way forward, not division.

There will never be enough laws passed nor safeguards established to stop someone that is bent of being racist, from doing what they want. No one can guarantee your personal safety. Likewise, one cannot legislate your personal attitude. It is only possible to put in place legislation to ensure consequences for wrong behaviors. It is possible use legislation to promote high morals in the society, however laws cannot change hearts or attitudes. Most countries in the western hemisphere have done that. We have crossed the point of no return.

When my family and I moved to Florida in 1999 I began working as the Drugs and Violence Prevention Coordinator with the Middle Schools in Hendry County. There was a gate at the entrance to the school that was closed at the end of the school day. One day I learned a very valuable lesson about perception when I drove up to the gate, looked at it and assumed that it was locked. Well, by all appearances I was locked out of my office. The gate was closed, and the lock was on the latch. I was impressed to look a little closer though. I took another look, and guess what? Someone had skillfully placed the lock in the latch and positioned it to look as if it was locked. I was not locked out of my office after all. It just looked that way. I experienced all the emotions of being locked out, just because I thought I was. I will never forget the lesson that I learned that day. I will always take the time to get a closer look and not just accept the common opinion about things.

We've come a long way, but now we need to teach about the brotherhood of all men. This will take on a new twist in the 21$^{st}$ century, because now everyone need to learn this lesson. It is not just a message for black or white. It's for all people, all shades and all ethnic groups. It is time for all sides to now get a clearer view. This will require everyone to come outside of their community.

There was a blind man who lived in a town called Bethsaida. This was in the days when Jesus walked the earth. The blind man cried out for help as Jesus walked by. His neighbors didn't mind if Jesus the miracle worker wanted to help Him, they just wanted him to keep quiet. The community knew him and rendered his case insolvable. They may have had good intentions and probably wanted to shield him from unrealistic expectations or they might have been more concerned about "getting theirs." Who knows? However, I've lived long enough to know that the good intentions of others might not be in my best interest. Good intentions can kill you.

The story continues with Jesus taking the man by the hand and leading him outside of the village. The community knew his problem, but for him to be healed he had to be willing to follow Jesus outside the community. In today's world traveling and moving is common and going outside ones' community may not seem like a big thing. But do you realize that in many ways this man was pulled outside of his comfort zone. He had to leave the people who loved him and knew him to be totally free. In his community he was simply blind Bart. That was all they knew about him. He was blind. They probably felt sorry for him and compensated him for his disability. He had been labeled. Everyone has a label and a nickname in the town where they grew up. I'm sure that most of the people whom I went to school with at Yallahs Primary School in St. Thomas, Jamaica would not even remember my name. But tell them my nickname. Ask them about "suga head." Just don't believe everything that you will hear!

Our community is our place of security. We know our place in it. It is a place where the rules are clear. The landmines, pitfalls and rites of passage are clear. We know what to expect from others and they know what to expect from us. In the community you can look at a person and tell who they are, where they are from and where they are going. You can pretty much tell everybody's family history. We know the good family, the worthless family and the thieves. We know how to talk to each other. No effort is required to say certain things. We can use dialects. We understand each other. We finish each other's sentences.

My mother was a very hard working single parent, and so during the summer she would send me from Kingston to my grandparents in the Montpelier, St. James (near Montego Bay). After a few summers, I knew which family in our little country village would fight you at the drop of a hat. I mean the whole family would. They would fight each other and turn around and beat you down to the ground. I also learned who were the rich ones, the "smart" ones and the ones everyone was betting on to succeed. Talk about stereotypes or profiling! No wonder Jesus had to bring this blind man outside his community to help him. I like the fact that Jesus led him. The possibilities are endless when Jesus leads us into the future.

The story of the blind man is very instructive. Mark, the writer, reports that Jesus "spit on his eyes and put His hands on him." The method was very unorthodox and seemed very unsanitary. It wasn't clean cut and formal. The formerly blind man looked up and said, "I see people, but they look like trees." For Jesus that was still not good enough. I like that about God, He wants us to be right, not just to get it right. The wrong perception is not just wrong; it's bad for us.

According to Mark, "Then (Jesus) put His hands on his eyes again and he was restored and saw everything clearly." Half-freedom is not freedom. There are no substitutes for complete freedom, complete healing, and complete restoration. The goal was not to "kinda see" nor "kinda-live." The goal of any movement that promises empowerment to people should not stop at political and economic power. Like Bartimaus, the goal must be about complete healing. Our forefathers did not endure slavery and all the past injustices for us to settle for what we have today. There is more. We must be able to find a sense of peace and settlement concerning the past, the present and our future.

There should be external and internal restoration so that the individuals might fulfill their potential in life. The work of Jesus was not completed by taking blind Bartimaus outside the community. The goal was not the journey itself. In fact, you don't have to take a single physical step outside of your bedroom to get outside your community. It's not about the distance you've travelled on the ground. It's the distance you've travelled in your heart. It's about your perspective. It is about your thinking process. It's about your growth. You can be a part of a community without being "owned" by the community. The days of tribalism are long gone. We are free. We are individually free. You are a free person.

In today's environment there is so much falsehood, so many half-truths, and so many politically correct ways of talking that it is not easy to see things clearly. I believe that despite the legal, political, economic, educational and social advances made across the western hemisphere by the descendants of African slaves, we have more steps to take. We need to get outside our community. I believe that it is time for us to embrace a more individualistic way of thinking in community. I'm not recommending that we replace the community with the individual, but I'm recommending that we place the value of the individual over the community. The community perception will change when individuals are changed. People really do change. I've met a few.

One of the reasons why the Bible was tightly censured for centuries, and continues to be censured in some countries today, is that it is perceived to be subversive. Those who desire absolute power and control over others will always despise the Bible. The Bible stirs up feelings of individual importance, and a supernatural basis of personal dignity and value. It points to a sense of purpose and destiny outside of the control of the government, tribe, community elders, dons, gang leaders, the well-heeled or those in charge. Those who read it claim a sense of moral certitude that seem narrow minded and un-teachable (read, un-able to be manipulated). Those who read and believe the Bible are often called rebellious, religious, selfish, prideful, and out of step, because they take the values of the Bible more seriously than the values of their earthly, and mortal superiors. The story of the progress of the descendants of African slaves in the western hemisphere cannot be repeated honestly without giving honor to Jehovah God, as revealed in the Holy Bible.

The Bible was the first textbook of the slaves. The continued study and revelation of the Word of God is also central to our future progress. My own family history has been profoundly and eternally improved because of the message of the Bible. My wife and I have been through storms and fires in our short journey of life. We have faced the name calling, the insults, the hurts, the embarrassments and offenses. This entire book could have easily been a documentation of the many offenses and wrongs committed against us individually, against our family, and we would need a few more books to list those injustices done to our mothers, grandparents and fore parents. And our story is not an isolated case. However, we can testify that one of the good news of the Bible is that like the three Hebrew boys in the Bible (Shadrack, Meshach and Abednego), you can go through the fire and come out without the smell of smoke. You can go through pain and not become bitter, angry or just "blowing smoke."

One of the key principles which we have learned is that there is a King of all kings and Lord of all lords. We have learned that the Almighty God is just, holy and fair. God is in control, and we should allow Him to take control. It is He who holds our future in His hands. His plans are good for us, and full of hope. I'm so glad I learnt this lesson early in life. It has helped me to relax in His arms and follow His path into my destiny. It has helped me to be more concerned about pleasing God than worrying about upsetting someone.

Another important principle is that of walking in forgiveness. My wife and I may share the same African heritage, but we are culturally different. We had to deliberately choose to build a meaningful relationship together. We had to deliberately choose to acknowledge and appreciate everyone we contacted, regardless of race or culture. We chose to keep an attitude of forgiveness available to others. We are really doing what we would like others to do to us.

We have learned that forgiveness is the key to building meaningful relationships. It must be a part of our daily lifestyle. Having a predetermined decision to be a forgiver is an outgrowth of the first principle: God is in control of me. It is not all up to me. My future is not up to others. If He has my future in His hands then I can forgive and receive forgiveness. I'm neither scared nor threatened by forgiving.

The negative effects of holding on to old wounds and old ways of thinking do not simply disappear with time. In fact given more time infection could set in. I was shocked to hear about gangs of black young men creating havoc in London, England. I was likewise deeply hurt when beautiful and friendly Montego Bay, Jamaica was called the murder capital of the world in 2017. Over 29 young adult gangs hunted and killed each other while holding their own neighborhoods hostage. We have a very serious problem among us, the descendants of African slaves.

Who can say that our young men and women are happy and peaceful? The violence, the weed and other drugs, the greed for money and power, the level of sexual immorality and fatalism is painful to watch. Many of our young men do not expect to live beyond 25 years old. It is time for a new perspective about the past and new perception of the future. This is not time for another round of Band-Aids. It's time for healing. It's time to forgive. It's time to live.

# Chapter 3

## A Higher Perspective.

The fishing is great in Charlotte County, Florida. The Peace River meanders lazily from miles inland emptying itself in the Charlotte Harbor. This brackish water is a fisherman's dream. This is the place to throw out a line or join up with an experienced captain. I like to fish, but I would never claim to be a fisherman. Fisher of men, maybe, but a fisherman, I'm not. That doesn't stop me though from telling my fishing stories. My sons may roll their eyes, but it is my story and I'm sticking to it! My fish stories get better every time I tell them. The fish is always bigger and I'm always smarter! Yes, it is amazing how two people can see the same thing, and even share the same experience and come away with totally different conclusions!

Everyone is entitled to his or her own perspective, but the truth is still the truth. The same is true concerning our history. Having a perspective about your history doesn't make it true. If we walk down to the corner of the street and ask the first person that we meet about their philosophy of life, most would look at us as if we were speaking a foreign language, but they certainly have their own views on life, the government, church, other people, etc. Our perspective on life is our philosophy of life.

Our perspective forms our perception of ourselves, of others and of the world around us. It tells us what to expect. It's the way we see things. Just because I see myself as a good fisherman doesn't make me one.

My wife tells the story of her own transformation in this area. She took a group of children from the after school program that she started to the local beach in Charlotte County. She arrived at the beach with her entourage ready to swim, but while she prepared to jump into the water she recalled feeling that all eyes on the beach were on her. She immediately realized that she was the only person with her shade of skin on the beach. Negative thoughts of her racial difference started coming to her mind. She had to choose her response. Would she leave, duck for cover, feel uncomfortable or just focus on her reason for being there? Well, because she had a new perspective, she concluded that the reason for the stares might be that the other beach goers were admiring the beauty of well-tanned skin. After all they were in the sun trying to get what she had! She went on to enjoy a great day at the beach with her students without worry about the reaction of others.

Our perception influences our attitude, which in turn determine our action. Our perspective of our history is the philosophy that we embrace to explain our history. The Bible says, "as a man thinks in his heart so is he" (Proverbs 23:7 KJV). What we think about our life experiences matter. What we think about other people matter. What we think about our potential, and our possibilities in life all matter. They come together to form our philosophy or perspective of life. It colors our responses, influences our decisions and shapes our future.

Your perspective is what you accept as the true relationship of one event to another. It is how you believe things relate or influence each other. Your perspective is also your worldview. In today's world we are often tempted to accept every opinion. We are also expected to have an opinion on so many things, and often without getting all the information. Not all perspectives are correct. North is not just the perspective of the one holding the compass!

True north exists; likewise, the correct perspective on each event exists. It is called a Godly perspective. There are no excuses for slavery or the injustices of the past. They were just plain wrong. When two people experience the same event from opposing side, it is possible, through God's grace, for both to become one. That is our goal.

God gives both individuals a higher perspective - the Godly perspective. Only God can make the offenders and the offended, one. Only through faith in Christ Jesus and obedience to the Holy Spirit can you and I be literally changed from brokenness to wholeness and from a hurting life to a healed life.

The Christian worldview is the only one that allows everyone to win. This is the "God-option."

Dr. Martin Luther King Jr. expounded this truth eloquently when he spoke on the topic of "loving your enemies." He said:

Certainly these are great words, words lifted to cosmic proportions. And over the centuries, many persons have argued that this is an extremely difficult command. Many would go so far as to say that it just isn't possible to move out into the actual practice of this glorious command. They would go on to say that this is just additional proof that Jesus was an impractical idealist who never quite came down to earth. So the arguments abound. But far from being an impractical idealist, Jesus has become the practical realist.

The words of this text glitter in our eyes with a new urgency. Far from being the pious injunction of a utopian dreamer, this command is an absolute necessity for the survival of our civilization. Yes, it is love that will save our world and our civilization, love even for enemies.

So, what is your perspective on your history? Is it a baggage that burdens your soul? Is it a cloud that hangs over your head? Is it a weapon in your hand against your fellow man? Is it a gavel in your hand and a legal document to hold in judgment over any one associated with the evils which you or your fore parents have suffered? It is true that many good people across the world have suffered much at the hands of cruel men. However, loving your enemies is still the best way forward.

In 1983, as a student at Christ For The Nations Institute in Dallas, Texas, I met several students from Yugoslavia. Today that country no longer exist. After years of control by a dictator, and many more years of hypocrisy and toleration of each other, the true perspective of the various ethnic groups came to the surface. It was sad to see Serbs, Croatians, and ethnic Albanians exact vengeance on each other for wounds and offenses which festered for decades, indeed for centuries. And, oh, what a carnage!

It is interesting to note that for decades the dictator manipulated each groups for his political benefit. Right in the middle of Europe on the dawn of the new millennium we heard of ethnic cleansing and genocide. As we say in Jamaica, "di story come to bump." In other words the "chickens came to roost." Hurt, bitterness and years of hypocrisy will eventually surface. Unsettled issues and unresolved offenses will not simply fade away with time. If not in this generation, then in the next: it will surface and demand justice.

The only way for injustices to be settled is for justice to prevail. Therefore, we must accept the fact that some issues are too massive, too far gone, the damage too intertwined, and so the just and wise thing to do is to forgive. To do otherwise would be to devalue the real impact of the offense. To do otherwise is like accepting a new bicycle from the guys who wrecked your car. How do you pay back someone for his or her heritage? What price can you put on their history? Some things can be done, and many things have been done. The logical final step is forgiveness. The best move is to take this issue to the higher court of God's justice. We have that opportunity today.

Are you familiar with 1 Timothy chapter 6 verse 10? It says, "The love of money is the root of all evil." And it is true. It is amazing how people can "put up" with people whom they literally despise just for the paycheck or the "bottom line." That is the love of money at work not a heart of love. That is not harmony. To tolerate someone as long as they are useful is neither good for them nor for you. How much money will it take to buy self-respect, peace and healing? Our nations exist in a state of false unity and false peace.

These questions trouble me: "What will happen when the money stops, and it is no longer necessary to pretend? What happens in a time of scarcity, recession or downright economic depression? If you had the upper hand, what would you do? What would you do to those who are the descendants of those who enslaved your fore-parents or of those who hurt you - if you could "get away with it?" What principles would guide your actions? What is in your heart? And what is your secret wish on this issue?

Here are some other important questions: What is the goal or desire of the African Diaspora now? Where are the current leaders leading us to? Is there one goal for everybody to line up behind? If so, what is it? Who sets it? What philosophical principles guides it? Who are the teachers? What is the vision? What do parents of African descent want to see happen to their children ten years from now? Where do you see yourself? What is your end game?

What if the earth remains for the next 100 years? Is our goal to go back to Africa? Is it to take everything from everyone who benefited from slavery? How would we know who benefited? What about those in Africa who benefited? What about our fore parents, children and relatives who are racially mixed? Is the goal reverse segregation of the races? Should we go back across the tracks and develop "our area" to compete with "theirs"? Is it to develop totally different economic bases? Or are we seeking a united future?

What was the perspective of Rev. Dr. Martin Luther King, Jr. and his dream anyway? Is hope still alive? Well, let me stop except to say that these are concerns that agitate our young people and dominate their thoughts. They need answers. These are the kinds of questions that moved me to write this book in the first place. I hope that by simply stating them, a long overdue conversation will be stirred up in homes, around water coolers, on the basketball, football, and soccer fields, in churches, at family reunion, and clubs everywhere. We must ask ourselves about how to solve this issue.

The things I am addressing are not confined to people of African descent. These principles and worldview applies to everyone everywhere, regardless of your background. If you or someone you love have been hurt, exploited, suffered injustice or offense in anyway, you should keep reading.

I was not there when slavery and all this mess started. Obviously you weren't either since you are reading this book. So I cannot completely trust the historical or political perspectives of the history of slavery, because, as my former history teacher from Australia once said, "every author has a certain slant." The absence of answers has been deafening. We need truth. It is time for healing. Our perspectives are often biased and very, very limited.

There are some who would immediately dismiss the Bible and its relevance in speaking to this issue. They attempt to do so by simply branding the Bible as the "white man's" book or as just plain irrelevant and outdated. I believe that this charge cannot be ignored, because it undercuts the source of wisdom and blocks the way to the fountain of living water. I know of too many young men across the USA, the Caribbean, and certainly in Jamaica who believed this argument and threw out the Bible, except for selected portions which seem to sanction their personal habits. When will they realize that they threw out the compass?

The divine origin of the Bible is supported by the text itself as well as by history and its influence on history. The historical and archaeological proofs of the authenticity of the Bible are just too many and too varied for listing here. Today there is hardly a language in the world where the Bible has not been written. The Bible has a place in human history all by itself. If ten copies of any ancient manuscript is found, the scientific community would immediately consider that manuscript an authentic classic. Well, over 5,000 manuscripts of the New Testament have been found so far, and most of them were written over a 300 year period by different people, and yet they agree. The oldest one goes back to the 4th or 5th century. Many more manuscripts of the Bible exist than of the writings of Socrates, Pluto or Alexander the Great. So why would you believe them, and doubt or ignore the Bible?

The proof is also in the pudding! Those who have truly lived their lives in the light of the teachings of the Bible have made the world a better place for you and me today. Have all followers of the Bible been perfect? No. The Bible recorded that even Christ Jesus had a Judas on His team. Judas betrayed every godly principle that he was taught.

So don't "throw out the baby with the bath water!" What will you replace it with? Have you truly examined the fruits of the alternative? You would have to use "dishonest" scales to say that the Bible does not meet and surpass the test of history and archaeology with flying colors. And so I submit to you the wisdom of the Biblical perspective on these matters.

The Lord Jehovah of the Bible has a proven track record of being unbiased and impartial. He has had the bird's eye view through this whole affair. He was there then, and He is here now. And, with the skill of a surgeon's gentle hand, He brings healing to the very root of the problem. There is a Divine perspective on slavery. There is a Divine perspective for our lives and future. It's time to capture that. God has something to say about the past and the present. His answer will give us hope and a clear vision for the future. 1 Corinthians 2 verse 11 says, *"Eyes have not seen, ears have not heard, neither has it entered in to the hearts of men the things that God has in store for them that love Him... But God has revealed them to us through His Spirit. For the Spirit searches all things, yes, the deep things of God... no one knows the things of God except the spirit of God. Now we have the Spirit who is from God, that we might know the things that are freely given to us by God."*

Slavery would still be going on openly and legitimately today if it were not for the obedient response of men and women operating under a Biblical worldview. Today we are glad to say that after centuries of existence, the African experience in slavery exposed this immoral and inhumane system and broke its stronghold. Thanks be to God, that something good came out of it. Slavery is no longer accepted as the normal treatment for prisoners of war, thieves, debtors and of people whom we just don't like. Those who practice slavery today, especially sex slavery, do so quietly and in the dark. It is no longer morally acceptable to own slaves anywhere in the world. That perspective only became true in these modern times.

The victories of people of African descent in the USA was based on universal moral and Godly principles and then codified by just laws. It motivated other disenfranchised people around the world to dream and work for their own civil and human rights. The suffering of Africans paved the way for others. God was there from start to finish, and He has a perspective on this historical fact. He also has a view of what the future should be. A recent Newsweek report of people enslaving their own countrymen right in the USA. Once again, a strong abolition movement is gathering momentum to fight this evil.

There was a time when I could not watch the great classic movies about the slave journey out of Africa, across the middle passage or life on the plantations without weeping and wondering; "Why, God? Why?" I could not celebrate the great victory of my fore parents to endure such suffering to make today possible for my generation. All I could see was the pain, the humiliation and the shame which was quickly followed by feelings of inferiority and anger all over again.

Some writers have said that this was God's way of getting Africans out of Africa so that He could give them an opportunity to hear the gospel, and for advancement. I strongly disagree with that view. Would we use that same premise for the Brits, who were literally barbarians before the gospel came? It is like saying that God so loved the world that He had to punish them to save them.

This view is inconsistent with common sense, and inconsistent with the teaching and the spirit of the gospel itself. Actually, it was Jesus Christ who was punished for the salvation of mankind. We do not need to be punished for our salvation!

Some believe that slavery happened because of the sins of West Africa. It is important to remember that God had a witness on the continent of Africa long before the 1400s. In Acts chapter 8 reference is made to an Ethiopian eunuch whom Phillip, the evangelist, baptized in either AD 62 or 63. He is reported to have founded the church in Ethiopia long before missionaries arrived. So God did not need the slave trade to introduce Himself or His ways to Africans.

God always has a witness of Himself in every culture. Romans 1:18-23 confirms this:

*For the wrath of God is revealed from heaven against all ungodliness and unrighteousness of men, who hinder the truth in unrighteousness that which is known of God is manifest in them; for God manifested it unto them.*

*For the invisible things of Him since the creation of the world are clearly seen, being perceived through the things that are made, even His everlasting power and divinity; that they may be without excuse: because that, knowing God, they glorified Him not as God, neither gave thanks; but became vain in their reasoning, and their senseless heart was darkened.*

*Professing themselves to be wise, they became fools, and changed the glory of the incorruptible God for the likeness of an image of corruptible man, and of birds, and four-footed beasts, and creeping things."*

I am always impressed by the way in which the Bible addresses mankind from all over the world. It is never condescending. There is not one message for the developed world and another for the under developed world. There is not one message for the rich and another for the poor. The ground is level at the foot of the cross. From the earlier passage there is a clear message that all men are naturally intelligent and innately knowledgeable enough to know God. We are smart enough and capable to choose to follow Him. If a person is "wise" enough to be aware of the need to worship something or someone, then they have all the capacity they need to know and worship the Creator. The basic principle is that the supernatural or invisible is confirmed by the presence of natural or visible things: trees, stars, sun, others human being, etc.

Psalm 19 also tells us that the heavens declare the glory of God, and the firmament (atmosphere of the skies) shows His handiwork. In other words, God uses the heavens and the things He created to communicate information about Himself to all the peoples of the earth. So God did not need to design slavery as a missionary tool to save the lost Africans.

There is nothing wrong with the trees, the ground, the water, the air, the ships, or the atmosphere of the continent of Africa. The people are the same everywhere - hearts with selfish motives, but hearts which can be changed because of the work of Jesus Christ through the power of the Holy Spirit. People everywhere love life. They want to prosper. They have the same desires as anyone else to prosper, to be fulfilled, to contribute to the welfare of mankind, to be happy, to have hope, to have children, to be loved, and to love. Like people across the globe, the love of money (or things used to trade in order to satisfy ones selfish desires) is the root of all evil. The bottom-line for the evil of slavery system was the bottom line. The main motivation was money and power. The tactic was to demean and objectify the African race to justify and cover over the real reason: more money.

A quick review of human history shows that slavery was not confined to the land of Africa nor to Africans. The Indian tribes enslaved their foes. The Muslim traders had slaves. Russians had slaves. Europeans enslaved each other. Asians had slaves and were enslaved. Indians had slaves and were enslaved. Slavery was used by both Africans and non-African people for centuries for a variety

41

of reasons. Throughout history there have been white, black, brown, red, yellow and all kinds of slaves. It was used as a punishment for debtors, prisoners of war and criminals. In some case, the slave owners were enslaving people of their own race.

Some say that people of African descent are really better off going through slavery, because it brought us into the new world. This assumption is ridiculous and false. This is obviously not a respectful, sensible nor Godly way to bring progress nor development to anyone. We are definitely better off, but it didn't have to happen that way.

I disagree with the concept that the end justifies the means. The fact that God works all things together for our good, does not mean that He approved or directed "all things" that happened. This was not one of God's plan to bring progress to Africa. How do we know? Because it runs contrary to the unconditional love of Christ which teaches us to love our neighbors as ourselves. Jesus commands us to go into all the world to preach and teach the Gospel, to bring freedom and liberty, not bondage and discrimination. It is totally inconsistent with Biblical teaching.

It is easy to assume that Africa is backward. In fact, even people of African ancestry still have a naive, patronizing, and often belittling attitude towards Africa, and Africans past and present. This is only a stereotype. Many also view Africans as somehow unable to develop their continent. They believe that the people of the continent are not as "advanced" as others on the Darwin's' human evolutionary chain. They view Africans with childish curiosity, because evolution puts Africans in the "prehistoric, ape-like stage." The Bible does not.

Do you know that the average African knows several languages and dialects? The average person in the Republic of Congo, for example, speaks French, Lingala, and/or Mumukutuba. That takes tremendous mental capacity. Another important fact is that Africa is not made up of one people group, one culture nor one nation, neither are all Africans necessarily one color.

A little research will show that Africa is not a nation, it is a continent made up of many nations. Africans before the days of slavery and Africans of today are multi-colored and multi-linguistic. Like Europe, America, Central and South America, the Middle East, the various nations and communities in Africa are at different levels of development. There are a variety of natural resources, vegetation and animals in the land. They have different cultures and customs. They do not all worship the same god.

There is no "mother god" of Africa. There is no utopian natural "authentic" life in Africa, more than anywhere else in the world. Majority of the people do not even sport the popular dreadlocks hairstyle. They comb their hair. They cut their hair. They wear beautifully well-tailored clothes. The African nations have had both good and bad kings, queens, major kingdoms and wars throughout their history, just like other places. Idolatry existed there just like any other place. We must also remember that most of the peoples on the African continent did not experience nor had anything to do with slavery.

Here are some statistics about this vast and wonderful continent taken from Patrick Johnstone's Operation World Handbook. At the beginning of the 21$^{st}$ century Africa had 10.4% of the world's population and over 3,000 ethno-linguistic people groups speaking 1,995 of the world's known languages. The total area of the African continent is 30,000,000 sq. km, which is about 16% of the earth's surface. At the time of this writing, a total of 55 nations exist across Africa. Many separate sub-Sahara Africa from Northern Africa, due to the heavy Islamic influence and cultural differences, but for all intents and purposes North Africans are Africans. There are at least 21 world-class cities in Africa and urbanization reached 45% at the beginning of the new millennium.

It is true that 32 of the world's 40 poorest countries are in Africa and that only 1.25% of the world's earnings are generated from this resourceful continent. However, the situation is like that because we are a mere 100 years removed from the "scramble for

Africa" by Europe. We are also less than 40 years removed from the days when the competing global influences of communism and capitalism clashed in Africa. Nations and their leaders were supported or removed based on their perceived benefit to the east or the west and not on their benefit to their own people. The people were the collateral damage. Then there was (and to some extent still) the near universal prejudice and economic stranglehold by Europe and the Americas of African nations. The aggressive funding and expansion of Islam's drive to become a powerful force in the world in this new Century have added to the internal challenges. The drive of China to tap into Africa's resources is having long lasting impact.

The nations of Africa are moving forward though. At the center of this resurgence is the Church. God's perspective when accepted and applied brings peace, harmony, knowledge, wisdom, equality, liberty, destiny, creative solution and a new sense of responsibility and prosperity. According to Patrick Johnstone of Operation World (1997 Edition.) stated:

Christianity is professed by over half of the sub-Saharan African population. This is the first time in history that the religious landscape of a continent has shown such dramatic changes. In 1980, African Christians were 8 million or 10% of the population. In 1990 this had risen to 275 million and 57% (of the population) and is likely to reach 396 million and 61% (of the population) by 2000."

The rise in commitment to Christ has undoubtedly resulted in increased development, increased hope, increased knowledge, increased motivation and increased prosperity of the countries and peoples of Africa. Now is the time for the people of African descent all over the world to work, support, serve, and become entrepreneurs, developers, and missionaries to Africa to support its spiritual, political, and economic development under the principles of the Word of God. The 21st century is Africa's century. We need to engage today's Africans and be open to also learn from their successes and failures. But how can we go if we are not healed?

So don't blame God for the problems of the "poor African" and smile when the "rich European" gets flooded. Although by now we must know that not all Africans are poor, and neither are all Europeans rich. And no one deserves to be flooded out.

It's okay if you realize, by reading this book, that you need a new perspective. The Apostle Peter needed a revelation to understand that God was not partial and that among every ethnic groups those who fears Him, and practice righteousness were accepted by Him. The Apostle Peter had to change his perspective and attitude towards others. "What God has cleansed you must not call common" (Acts 10:15). This change does not happen automatically. Sometimes, even after God forgives us it is hard to forgive others.

I have discovered where the blame for the pain of slavery lies. It is the devil that destroys, enslaves and imprisons people. He is the one that comes "to kill, steal, and destroy" (John 10:10). He is the master schemer behind the horrors of slavery, prejudice, racism, discrimination, and subjugation. He is the one to blame. He is the one keeping the pain alive.

The mass enslavement of millions of West Africans was not the devil's first and only destructive blow. Many wicked and unjust events took place before then, and continue today. The enslavement of millions of West Africans is our story and so it impacts us the most. As hurtful as this sounds, the truth is that the Atlantic slave trade was just another trade in human traffic. The only difference might be that the traders came in bigger boats, looked different and left for the other side of the world. I'm sure that before that slaves were regularly swapped among African tribes. It was nothing new, just another trade opportunity and new partners. I also believe that the very moment the first ship set sail for Africa; God immediately set in motion a plan to bring victory out of the vice.

Here are some scriptures that further reveal God's heart on the matter. It shows that He really is able to cause all things to work together for good.

*"For God so loved the world that He gave His only begotten Son that whosoever believes in Him should not perish but have everlasting life."* John 3:16.

His goodwill was extended towards all men through Jesus Christ. The intent is to stop the destruction.

*"Lord is not slack concerning His promises as some would count slackness, but is long-suffering toward us, not willing that any should perish but that all should come to repentance."*
1 Peter 3: 8

*"No temptation (testing) has overtaken you, except such as is common to man, but God is faithful, who will not allow you to be tempted beyond what you are able, but with the temptation will also make a way of escape, that you may be able to bear it."*
1 Corinthians 10:13

*"The devil comes to kill, steal and destroy, but I have come that you might have life and that more abundantly."* John 10:10

*"...God was in Christ reconciling the world to Himself, not imputing their trespasses to them, and has committed to us the word of reconciliation. Now then, we are ambassadors for Christ, as though God were pleading through us: we implore you on Christ's behalf, be reconciled to God."* 2 Corinthians 5: 19, 20

God is not a destroyer. He has never been and never will be. God is not a slave master. He has never been and never will be. He is the liberator - has always been and will ever be. Evil men have tried to twist the truth to their own wicked ends, but the Spirit of Christ never endorsed, supported nor gave any measure of credibility to any form of oppression, repression, slavery, nor wicked act. It is the thief that kills, steals and destroys.

The Bible is filled with examples of how God operates to liberate people. God looks for someone willing to listen and follow His ways, then He quickly moves to dismantle the prevailing bondage. History is filled with testimonies of this truth. Godly men and women continue to make the world a better place today.

God did not give anyone the green light to engage in slavery nor in any form of oppression of others. Yes, some, not all, but some leaders in the church gave it their "blessing" and caused confusion about God's position on slavery, but the system of slavery was never blessed by God. That water was far from holy. Later many of those same organizations repented and rejected their biases and erroneous teachings after an honest, and unbiased reading of the Bible.

Many believe that in order for the Almighty God to indeed be truly Almighty, then everything that happens on the earth is either allowed or permitted by Him. This view suggests that God was either a co-conspirator or at least a silent bystander. This logic flies in the faces of the Word of God. It may sound like a comforting position and an easy way to make sense of the tragedies of earth, but only the Word of God can truly tell us how God operates.

Let's look at John 3:16 *"For God so loved the world that He gave His only begotten Son, that whoever believes in Him should not perish but have eternal life."* If it was God intention for His will to be accomplished on the earth without human participation, then there would be no need for the coming of Jesus Christ, no need for His vicarious death and glorious resurrection, and no need for me or anyone else to tell this good news. If God always wins, then He would not have taken this initiative to stop the perishing. To "permit" means to either start it, give it verbal or silent green light or allowing it to continue when you could have stopped it.

Where was God's "permit office" for those who wanted to enslave their fellowmen?

The very essence of being human is that we have a God-given ability to choose good or evil. By giving man this ability God is not endorsing, setting, preplanning and pre-engineering all of man's actions. Man has been given the capacity to be creative, like His creator. Man is a freewill agent.

The bottom line is that during this dispensation or season of time, the Almighty and Just God also abides by just principles. He has given man the freedom of choice, and hence the consequences of it. In the same way Jesus Christ laid aside His deity and became a man. God has given man this season of choice. It is also a season when the work of sin in the earth and the activity of the tempter is moving with full speed. The Almighty will bring all men, Satan and all the tempters into judgment for their decisions and action. Every knee will bow, as the scripture says.

I have lived long enough to know that not everyone who shows up in the name of God was actually sent by Him. We can find out if they are of God by considering their spirit, attitude, motive, and the results of their word/message. Galatians 5:22 clearly tells us that the "fruit" (or evidence of the presence and involvement) of the Holy Spirit is manifested in our interaction with others. Is there love, joy, peace, long-suffering, kindness, goodness, faithfulness, gentleness, and self-control?

The evidences of the flesh is also clear, because it is influenced by the unclean spirit of satan *"...adultery, fornication, uncleanness, lewdness, idolatry, sorcery, hatred, contentions, jealousies, outbursts of wrath, selfish ambitions, dissensions, heresies, envy, murders, drunkenness, revelries, and the like; of which I tell you beforehand, just as I also told you in time past, that those who practice such things will not inherit the kingdom of God"* (Galatians 5:19-21).

So let's put the blame where it rightly belongs. It is not a "flippant statement" to say that the devil was involved. It was the devil that tempted our forefathers to stray from the knowledge and worship of the true and living God. It was the devil that stirred the heart of those who came with the ships to West Africa with greed, heresies, prejudices, and the love of money. It was the devil that stirred up hatred and tribal warfare so that one tribe would sell the other. It was the devil that directed the Muslim traders deep into the interior of Africa. They were the middle men in this wicked scheme. It was the devil in the wicked acts of the middle passage where people were packed like bananas in the deep dark holes of the ships. Many were simply thrown overboard if a storm came and the ships were too heavy. It was the devil all along, and it is still the devil today seeking to extend the damage deep into as many generations as we allow him to. We allow his wicked intentions to success. We give him permission to hurt us.

Our true enemy has no skin color. He is not a man. He doesn't care about racial issues. He doesn't care about our history; he's only intent on our misery. He is afraid of our destiny, and, so, if binding us to the hurts of our history will hinder us from fulfilling our destiny that is exactly what he will do. He wants to win against God at our expense.

The enemy causes the pain then stirs up the anger over the pain. He then returns with bitterness and un-forgiveness, because those responses will lead to self-destruction and generational bondage. He knows that bitterness dries up the bones (Proverbs 17:22).

> *Let all bitterness, and wrath, and anger, and clamour, and evil speaking, be put away from you, with all malice*
> *(Ephesians 4:31)*

An article in the Newsweek magazine (September 24, 1990) stated that, "healthy thinking may eventually become an integral aspect of treatment for everything from allergies to liver transplant and prevention of disease." In his book, *A More Excellent Way*, Pastor Henry Wright asserts that unforgiveness is the number one hindrances to healing.

The devil hates you and all your children. He dances on the graves of those whom he lured into his wicked traps. He extends hurts and seeds of unsettledness to steal the potential of as many generations as possible. He is a trickster and he is constantly scheming to keep mankind out of step with the truth and out of step with inner peace. This is a spiritual war manifested in the physical, mental, and financial realm.

Spiritual warfare requires a spiritual approach. There are some deep spiritual issues that must be dealt with before you can take advantage of your civil, economic, and political rights. The first step in this battle is to identify the real enemy. You need to do this or you'll spend your lifetime beating the wind.

Who is the thief? Who is stealing your future? Who meddled in your history? Who is your enemy? Who is the enemy of all mankind? Name the enemy. It's the defeated devil who is constantly peddling false perspectives and stirring up division among people to steer us all down the path of death.

Ephesians chapter 6 verse 12 reminds us that *"We do not wrestle against flesh and blood [so much for penalizing people because of their roots] but against principalities and powers, against the rulers of darkness of this age, against spiritual host of wickedness in heavenly places."*

A prayer walk is where a group of Christians walk through a neighborhood to pray over the homes and the community in general. At one of those events in Clewiston, Florida, a dear Christian lady remarked that she was trusting God to break all curses over her family, because if she did not, it would be harder for the next generation to do so. She is an African-American woman of God, and she was right. That statement went under my skin and lodged into my heart. It provoked me to consider the legacy I was leaving for my children. Our inheritance includes the conditions of our soul, and not just our political, cultural and financial positions.

What unchallenged spiritual stronghold will you leave for your children to deal with? What backward diabolic thinking pattern will be passed on to them? What perception will influence their worldview? It is time to stand and say, "STOP, IN THE NAME OF JESUS."

I believe that the devil can recognize divine potentials and tell God's intent. The Apostle John was exiled on the Isle of Patmos, when he wrote the book of Revelation, the last book of the Bible. He wrote about that day around the throne of God when people from every tribe and nation will gather, and, in their own unique culture, contribute to the worshipping of the God of Heaven. Every people group on the earth, have a unique role to play and a unique melody to add to the symphony of heaven. The fallen angel, and fired worship leader knows this, and I believe that he is working overtime to disrupt it. He will use slavery, wars, and famines. Then after freedom comes, he will use riches, greed, lust, bitterness, vengeance, pride, and deep hurts to keep you from your full potential. He is after the potential. He is after your worship.

One of his prime strategies is to plant seeds of hopelessness, fear and distrust of God in the hearts of men. He seduces man into an anti-God perspective about the present and past. Beware of this spirit of the anti-Christ. It tells us that the work of Christ was not enough to fix our problems today. Every human being who is successful in fulfilling his or her divine destiny literally mortifies the enemy. He hates to see you become what God created you to be. I say go ahead and be that anyway. Live life God's way. Worship Jehovah with all of your strength! It's time to fulfill your divine destiny. Go for it!

## Chapter 4

## The Issues We Face Today

Why were over 335 people murdered in St. James, Jamaica in 2017? Jamaica is not in a civil war, and yet in a nation with 2.7 million people, 1665 people were killed in 2017. When two men were gunned down outside the Montego Bay airport, the government quickly slapped a state of emergency on the entire parish. For several months Police and soldiers struggled to re-establish order in the once quiet and friendly St. James. Ravaging gangs of young men of African roots (black men) were wreaking havoc, despair, death and destruction on their own neighborhoods, cities and nation. The average age of the horde of gangsters is 17. To many of them, an old man is 25 years old. They are angry, and unwilling to come under anyone's control. What is going on?

On January 1, 2001 the members of the main Catholic Church in Castries, on the island of St. Lucia, gathered for their annual New Year Eve celebration. It wasn't long before two young men, dressed in white gowns and sporting flowing dreadlocks, with clubs and a machete charged into the sanctuary threatening to "burn down Babylon." The newspaper reported that when it was all over, an Irish nun who had served on the Island, as a missionary for 42 years, was dead and several others wounded. The Church building was partially burned. What happened? Why did those men resort to such violence? What was going on in their minds?

Cincinnati, Ohio, was a ghost town for many nights in April 2001. Hundreds were arrested and a curfew was imposes by the Mayor. The city was burning. Windows were broken, cars were destroyed and shops looted as hundreds of rioters poured into the street to protest the shooting of a 19 year old unarmed African-American young man by a white policeman. What was at the root of the violence that erupted in Cincinnati, Ohio and Castries, St.

Lucia? I believe that it is more than citizen response to police work or two crazy young men high on marijuana (ganja).

Similar protest have erupted in Ferguson, Missouri, in Baltimore, in Dallas and on several College campuses. Movements like "Black Lives Matters" and "Hands Up Don't Shoot" refuse to go away quietly into the night. These incidents keep popping up in separate places, but they share a common root.

Incidents like these are regularly featured on the news. They define the very culture of being black in the 21st century as being angry, "with a chip on the shoulder," gangster, hip-hop, dancehall, after money, sex and self-gratification now, agitated, separatist and wanting to punish anyone involved with past and present wrongs - from slavery to the latest offense. We can't allow these caricature to take root.

The frequent protests and flare ups in neighborhoods, cities and nations are indeed manifestations and warnings of a deeper problem. I believe that it is a consequence of the continuing pain and unsettledness bubbling up in the hearts of many people; young and old. They feel disrespected, dis-connected, isolated and unaccepted. The history of racism, prejudices and discriminations may have been legally or political dealt with, but, for many, it is not yet settled on the personal level. Many are yet to be healed. Their perspective on life is fueling their action.

Getting beyond the wounds of the past is made more difficult because of today's struggles and challenges; whether real or perceived. Consequently, today's struggles and yesterday's problems have become indistinguishable. New aggressive groups are being formed to deal with present day issues, but when you listen to their narrative or read their manifestos you will hear a rehearsal of the same unresolved racial issues. When past problems are mixed in with the present justice concerns, it is easy to be despondent and to conclude that nothing has changed.

It is quickly becoming too much to handle. We're at a critical point. It's that dangerous stage of a festering wound. It doesn't take much for an infection to flare up. I believe that the jury is still out in the USA and the west. Things could go either way – harmony or disharmony. We will come together or break apart. The status quo is untenable.

We have entered a new millennium, and we are still not healed. Is it even possible to be healed, you might ask? The words of Malcolm X (El Hajj Malik El Shabazz) explains the dominant perspective of today: "If you stick a knife nine inches into my back and pull it out three inches that is not progress. Even if you pull it all the way out, that is not progress. Progress is healing the wound, and America hasn't even begun to pull out the knife."

If we believe that "America hasn't begun to pull out the knife" then our perspective, our attitude and our actions will be affected. The question is whether or not we have made any progress? If we teach that Malcolm X is still right, then our young people will react accordingly. Who wants to walk around with a knife stuck in their back?

The evidence of brokenness is everywhere. The unsettled issues concerning slavery, ethnicity, and ancestry are too much of a heavy burden for the next generation to carry. We cannot ignore the problems any more. It's like a nagging toothache. It may subside for a while, but everyone knows that it is just lying below the surface waiting to flare up again. We cannot pass them off or blame others any longer. It is time for personal action.

I was told to never back a cat into the corner, because he will come at you with everything and anything he has. It's called the fight or flight instinct of self-preservation. If you feel backed into a corner you would come out swinging. Unfortunately, the people who suffer the most would be those closest to you. The irony is that the ones whom you really want to "feel your pain" isn't even aware of your meltdown! And what can they do by knowing or "understanding?" This sense of hopelessness, disillusionment and desire to "teach society a lesson" is at the root of many violence and gang involvement today.

Millions of dollars have been spent discussing and diagnosing the reason why "the cat is in the corner." Millions are spent at conferences and strategy sessions about social justice issues. Lofty intervention plans, work programs, career development strategies and educational opportunities have been carefully and lovingly designed and funded. But no one shows up. The program directors have to beg the people they are serving to help them to get a good attendance to keep the programs going. Trillions have been spent incarcerating men, women and children. They are placed in holding cages while society hopes that they will simply calm down. Billions more are spent on all manner of legal and illegal drugs to sedate the "cats", but the "cats" won't stop coming.

Many of our young men lack the motivation and support to take advantage of opportunities to prosper. Too many of them are in prisons, and we should not just blame the courts for that. The cycles of poverty, fatherless-ness and other generational bondages must be broken. We know deep inside that something is wrong.

The lyrics of the popular music filling the cars, parties and barber shops trade in the violence, anger, rage, immorality and pain in our communities. I saw a CD with the angry face of an otherwise pretty African-American young lady with one word printed at least ten times over the front of the CD: hate, hate, hate…. The words of many popular artists and social commentators often perpetuate fear, anger, pain, disillusionment, disappointment, unsettledness, entrapment and disconnection. The treatment of our women is beyond depressing. They repeat the same old racial hurts of yesteryear as if they happened yesterday.

I often wonder whether the songs are a reflection of the community, or just another blatant plan to profit from the pain. Are drug dealers helping people of African heritage to get over the pain or are they just bloodsuckers? I believe they are the modern day slave masters and slave catchers. They profit on the back of anyone they can use. Like Nimrod, the ancient godfather of the city of

Babel, they hunt the souls of men, robbing them of their divine destiny and enslave them in their group. They prey on the pain of their own brothers and sisters. They are not afraid nor reluctant of using the unsettled pain from our history of slavery to their benefit. A struggle is under way for the very heart and soul of this generation. The future is at stake. It is time for change?

The problem is not simply anger. These things are the fruits of an infected tree. There is a root. I believe that the root is that the issues concerning the history of slavery and discrimination have not been settled on the personal level. I believe that the root is un-forgiveness of the pain of slavery and discrimination.

As people of African heritage we must re-evaluate our current approaches to our problems. What was done in the past did not complete the job, and it's not working today. This is not a call to simply become a Christian and then, voila, all our problems will be over. You might "prayed through", "prayed about it", "prayed for them" or "given it to the Lord" and still end up without the breakthrough, if you are not healed.

If the unsettled issues around the mistreatment which you have suffered at the hands of others is too hard even for God to solve, then you will end up with a deep-seated sense of hopelessness and depression. The Bible says, "Hope differed makes the heart go sick" (Proverbs 13:12). Many are feeling depressed because their reality does not match the expectation of life after the civil rights marches, the sit-ins, the vigils and the much celebrated political and legislative victories. The fact is that although many prayers have been answered. The next level requires a different approach.

People of African heritage tend to have a very large threshold for pain. The methods which we use to survive from day to day are simply amazing. We are masters of submerging our true feelings and just "keep on trucking" or "just hanging in there." We keep on smiling although our heart is broken into a thousand pieces. We just get up the next morning and go to work! However, this approach does not cause the hurt to go away; it only delays the reaction and makes it worse. It does not solve the problem. It leads to more problems and usually spills over out on the wrong people; those closest to us.

We also know how to resign ourselves to "fate" and "the powers that be." People who do this will often say, "it's the system" or "it is what it is" or "a so it set." This is a sure death wish, not just for you, but also for your children's children.

I do not believe that we should ignore the unsettled issues and just pray through. No! The Bible teaches us to deal with the issue, not to simply pray for grace to bear up under what could be resolved. A great preacher said that quite often while we are waiting on God, He is waiting on us. The Bible says that as much as you have the ability, be at peace with all men. I believe that we have not exhausted our capacity to be at peace. God has given us the ability to do better than this. Our fore parents suffered for a better outcome than this.

It is very easy to get caught up in feelings of self-pity. Statement such as: no other group has suffered as much; no other group has paid a higher price nor suffered such great exploitation, are often used to describe the story of people of Africa heritage. The truth is that every nationality, every racial and language group have had times of pain, exploitation, discrimination, and victory. There are differences in the details, but suffering is suffering, and pain is pain and all human tragedies should be respected. We can certainly learn from others. There is more to be done. We need to shed light on these issues, confront them, and find healing.

There is no need for comparisons about who had the worse deal. It is easy to think that your history is the only one with slavery as a part of it. It is also easy for some to simply dismiss the issues that many people of African descent are struggling with as old news or old wounds. Some will say, "Just get over it." Others say, "Look how much money we have given to your community already." However, money cannot fix this one. It is not that easy nor that simple.

There are some things that money cannot buy. Money cannot heal a wounded heart nor give a young man a true sense of hope and purpose for living. Money cannot erase history. This is a job for a heart specialist not law enforcement nor a social worker nor a politician. This is spiritual work. Malcolm X was right, "progress is healing the wound."

The important and relevant issue though, is not the cause of the wound, but where can healing be found? The one responsible for the wound is not capable of healing it. The wounded person cannot self-heal. I suggest that you look at the Bible and check out the experience of Israel. The principles taught in the Bible are historically, politically, economically, philosophically, and morally sound. They can help you find healing so that you can go forward and experience your destiny in God. You have a purpose to fulfill. Don't put it off any longer. It's time to turn the search light within, lift your eyes upward and begin to deal with the issues that have delayed your destiny. We have inherited much blessings, but we have unfinished business.

## Our Fathers Fought For Liberty
by
James Russell Lowell

Our Fathers fought for liberty
They struggled long and well
History of their deeds can tell- but did they leave us free?
Are we free from vanity?
Free from pride and free from self?
Free from love of power and pelt
From everything there beggarly?

Are we free from stubborn will?
From our hate and malice small
From opinion tyrant thyrall
Are none of us our own slaves still?
Are we free to speak our thoughts
To be happy and be poor
Free to enter heaven's door
To live and labor as we ought?

Are we then made free at last
From the fear of what men say
Free to reverence today,
Free from the vacuum of the Past.

Our Fathers fought for liberty
They struggled long and well
History of their deeds can tell-
but did they leave us free?

## Chapter 5

## Lessons from Israel

The Bible recorded that when Jacob led his fifty descendants into Egypt to survive the famine, he did not know that it would have resulted in a four hundred-year stay. They entered as a small group but left as a small nation. It is an interesting story with many similarities to the story of African slaves and their descendants. To start with both were sold into slavery by their brothers.

The Israeli story started with Joseph being kidnapped and thrown into a holding pit, then into a prison after being falsely accused by his master's wife. Joseph eventually became the second most powerful man in the land of his captivity. Amazingly, at the end of the story, we discovered that Joseph was in the right place at the right time to rescue his famished family. The very same brothers who sold him came to Egypt to seek food. He was in the right place to help them. He opened a great door of opportunity for his family. They all moved to Egypt. And they prospered, because Joseph chose to forgive his brothers.

Joseph's perspective was very unique. He had ample opportunities to take revenge and teach his brothers a lesson. He blessed them and helped them instead. He operated from the viewpoint that "what (his brothers) meant for bad, God meant for good" (Genesis 50:20). This attitude or approach to life no doubt influenced the lifestyle of the Israelites while they lived among the Egyptians. They had a winning attitude even when the cards were stacked against them. Their faith was in a higher authority. So they prospered.

It is important that you understand this principle, because it is relevant to our life today. Joseph acknowledged the unfairness and evil of his experiences, but he also realized that God had a plan which superseded human injustices, and earthly inequalities.

60

Sometimes we give other people - man, nations, culture - too much say so and too much influence over our thinking, and our attitude, and eventually our lives. Don't give free rent space in your head to anyone. We can become so worried about people's reaction that we suppress the very will of God.

Joseph was able to help his needy brothers by walking in forgiveness, embracing his opportunities and maturing into his purpose. Egypt had a culture that was anti-truth, anti-god, and was definitely anti-Jewish, yet he focused on keeping his heart pure — not settling political or historical scores. It is so easy to get caught up in "the struggle" that you forfeit your true potential.

When Joseph had the opportunity to "rub it in" by messing around with Potiphar's wife, he decided to do things the right way. He must have settled some issues internally concerning his character. He said, "How can I do this great wickedness and sin against God" (Genesis 39:9)? He carried no chips on his shoulders. He had no secret desire for revenge. There was no place in him for a spirit of lust, inferiority, bitterness, vengeance, anger, hopelessness nor rejection. He did not see himself as a minority; he saw himself simply as Joseph. He never stopped being a member of the minority race or group, but he did not operate like a minority. He refused to dwell in categories set by others. He had settled the issue of his identity. He received his identity from God. He was more concerned about honoring God than with anything else in life.

Genesis 50:15-20 gives us an insiders' view of how Joseph dealt with those who did him wrong:

> And when Joseph's brethren saw that their father was dead, they said, "Joseph will peradventure hate us, and will certainly requite us all the evil which we did unto him."
>
> And they sent a messenger unto Joseph, saying, "Thy father did command before he died, saying, 'So shall ye say unto Joseph, <u>Forgive, I pray thee now, the trespass of thy</u>

<u>brethren, and their sin; for they did unto thee evil'</u> and now, we pray thee, forgive the trespass of the servants of the God of thy father."

And Joseph wept when they spake unto him. And his brethren also went and fell down before his face; and they said, "Behold, we be thy servants."

And Joseph said unto them, "Fear not: for am I in the place of God? But as for you, ye thought evil against me; but God meant it unto good, to bring to pass, as it is this day, to save much people alive. <u>Now therefore fear ye not: I will nourish you, and your little ones."</u>

<u>And he comforted them, and spoke kindly unto them.</u>

Like Joseph, we can find our present identity in the place of God. I'm with God.

Who defines you? Pain and persecution will reveal the true source of your identity. Joseph was not defined by Egypt nor the family who betrayed him. He operated from a higher perspective that enabled him to be bigger than his successes and the pain which he suffered, and so can you. Pain exposes the content of one's character. Godly character will outlast pressure any day. Joseph would have lost his opportunity to fulfill God's will for his life if he did not guard his character during times of success and suffering. You will not have what it takes to help those closest to you unless you walk in forgiveness.

Joseph knew where he was going. He wanted the future that God had for him. At the end of his life, he instructed the children of Israel to take his bones with them when they left Egypt. Joseph was a wise man. The man who helped to make Egypt prosper was not a "sell out" after all. He had foresight. He was no "Uncle Tom." He was not an accommodator, as some would call anyone who seemed to prosper or "get ahead" today. He believed God's report about his history and took advantage of the opportunities before him. He did it God's way. You can too.

Years later the Egyptians forgot about Joseph. The success and sheer numbers of the Israelites intimidated them. The Jews had also turned away from God's ways, and by so doing they basically set themselves up for failure. So the Egyptians took advance of their vulnerability and enslaved them. God finally raised up Moses to lead them out to freedom. Actually, God's goal was not just to give them freedom. He never meant for them to remain as permanent residents of Egypt. They had become comfortable and forgotten the plan. The Lord led them out to lead them into the fulfillment of His promises to their forefathers. They finally concluded that it was better to fulfill their destiny than to live to feed the Egyptians and keep the system going.

The famine that led them to Egypt lasted for only seven years, and yet they stayed for 430 years! God's heart is often broken because our cry for freedom is often temporary. He knows the difference. A passion for living free is a great treasure. I encourage you to nurture that. There is no higher purpose in life than to fulfill one's purpose.

After many struggles, much fighting and opposition, the Israelites were victorious. They returned to Canaan to fight and possess the land promised to them. Several years passed as 12 judges and 39 kings ruled the new nation. An interesting cycle can be seen over this period of time. Melton Short, in his book *The Old Testament Made Simple*, called it the "Five Step Cycle." Israel would stray away from God, and then an enemy nation would oppress them. They would cry to God for deliverance, and God would raise up a deliverer, and then they would serve God faithfully for a while before starting the cycle all over again. This cycle happened seven times during the 400 years period of the judges.

History is truly His-story. A quick look at history shows that people who refuse to live by the principles of God's word will suffer oppression. It's the law of nature. The enemy of man (satan) is always waiting for us to step out from under the Divine protection. Once that happens, he is then able to use other people who are under his control to do his dirty job. God is not doing this to people. We are doing it to ourselves. God sets in place the laws of sowing and reaping. God gave us freedom of choice. If the rain is falling and someone covers you with an umbrella, is it his fault if you deliberately step out from under the umbrella into the rain? Like us, Israel was well aware that a just God must also be an impartial judge. They chose to rebel against God's way of living.

God has no pleasure in the death or destruction of those who reject Him. In fact, I believe that it is because of God's love for us why He is so persistent in his attempt to communicate with us and minister to us. He knows much more than we do. He cares. He knows what is around the corner.

In 1998 I visited Paris for the finals of the World Cup Soccer competition. Jamaica was in the World Cup for the first time, and so I led a group of students on a short-term mission's trip. We were all stunned when soldiers suddenly showed up at the Charles de Gaulle Airport and drove us out of the terminal. We had to run outside without our luggage. Their rifles were drawn. They demanded that we obey. It was not a drill. There was no polite encouragement to leave. They demanded immediate response, and I am glad they did, and we did. We were also very glad that the package which they found and blew up was not a bomb. They knew more than we did. They had the knowledge and authority to do their job. Likewise, God is very capable in His divine role as God. Let him be your God. Trust Him.

The Bible clearly teaches that the Creator of heaven and earth desires that we should not worship other god or idols. Idolatry refers to any focus of our faith and hope other than our Creator, the Lord God, Jehovah. Our cultures have become filled with idolatry. It existed in Egypt, in Canaan, among the Israelites, in Rome, in Asia, in Europe, in the Americas, and among the peoples of Africa. Idolatry still exists today.

Sin does not mean living a western lifestyle. Sin does not mean living an eastern lifestyle either. Sin is not a lifestyle or culture. It is not a cultural issue; it is about worship. It is a matter of the heart. Idolatry is sin. Many may call idol worship or ancestral worship a form of respecting our ancestors or protecting the environment. Some may call it cultural heritage. However, there is a difference between respecting and honoring your heritage and making a religion out of it. I support respecting and honoring our ancestors.

God's judgment on idolatry is impartial and is the same today as it was centuries ago. The consequence of national or communal agreement to practice idolatry is oppression from others. The principle is simple: you will be ruled by the one you worship. The one to whom you give authority will take authority over you. If God did not spare Israel from exploitation by their enemies when they strayed from Him, certainly everyone is vulnerable. Regardless of your racial, cultural, or national heritage, the devil will do all kinds of evil against you as soon as you step out of God's protective covering. Personal and national oppression increases when God is excluded, and they come under the authority of Satan. The story of Israel is a clear example of this principle.

The Israelites forgot the important lessons about God during their sojourn in Egypt and through the wilderness. Their hearts were not committed to developing a personal relationship with Him even after 40 years of wandering in the wilderness. They had religion, but not a relationship with their God. The people knew the works of God, but they did not know His ways. Consequently, they were not prepared for the freedom that they received.

They listened to the wrong messengers over and over again. They rebelled and did what was right in their own eyes. They tried to adopt the lifestyle and perspective of the very nations which they overthrew. The result was that Babylon, led by Nebuchadnezzar, raided Israel and destroyed the beautiful

Solomon's temple, which was the heart and soul of Israel. They
went back into oppression. They could not believe it. They were
devastated. The harps were put away and sorrow filled their lives.
"How could they sing the Lord's song in a strange land?"

Egypt is therefore a symbol of a people in bondage, but
Babylon is a symbol of confusion. These two places hold symbolic
meanings for us today. If we compare the experience of the people
of African descent here in the Western hemisphere to that of
Israelites, I would say that we left our "Egypt" between 1830 -
1870s when slavery was abolished in the USA and most European
colonies around the world. It was even later for some groups.
Some might even argue that they did not leave "Egypt" until the
enactment of the United States' civil rights laws of the 1960s.
However, even using that time frame, we are now over the 40-year
mark - one generation. We are in the season of a new generation.

I believe that we are in the "Babylonian" era, if our
comparison to the Jewish experience holds true. The Babylon
scene is quite different from the one in Egypt. It was a confusing
time. In Egypt the Israelites were subdued into slavery away from
their homeland. They were not a nation then; they had no national
identity, just family connections. As slaves in Egypt, they were the
full concern of their slave master.

During the Babylonian oppression Nebuchadnezzar
conquered Israel, took those who were the brightest and of greatest
potential away to Babylon. In fact, it is referred to as a captivity
rather than enslavement. Nebuchadnezzar destroyed all the leaders,
but left the people in their own land. He gave them a measure of
self-government. They could work and farm, but they would have
to support Babylon with high taxes. They could never fully benefit
from their efforts. He also ensured that all leaders remained under
his control.

It is depressing to feel like an outsider in the very place that
you call home. But that is exactly where we are today. Many feel
like strangers in the land of their birth. The population of our

prisons systems, the economic and social condition of the Caribbean Islands and many other nations, are clear indications that we are in a state of confusion. Bob Marley was right about the oppression of Babylon, but wrong about who they were, and the answers we need. The wrong kind of leader only leads to more confusion and greater oppression. And we are experiencing Bob Marley's legacy today. We need true prophetic voices.

While Israel was in Babylon, much like today, many prophets arose. They meant well. They probably had good intentions. They were spiritual but did not have His current word about the problem. The current word is important. "Man shall not live by bread alone (or like we say in Jamaica 'breads - money') but by EVERY WORD THAT PROCEEDS FROM THE MOUTH OF GOD" (Matthew 4:4 NKJV) There is a "proceeding" word. There is a word from God that gives us wisdom, clarity and direction on how to proceed. It is a healing word for the future. It gives light and hope. It clears up the confusion.

Jeremiah is considered one of the Major Prophets in the Old Testament. His ministry ran from 626 - 586 B.C. covering the period before and during the Babylonian captivity. His perspective was very unpopular and politically incorrect, but he was actually right. Majority opinion is not always the right one. This is true regardless of one's ethnicity.

In Jeremiah chapter seven, with King Nebuchadnezzar marching towards Israel, Jeremiah made bonds and yokes and sent them to the king of Judah basically telling him that Israel would lose the war. I wonder what it was like to report that to his people. Can you imagine the inner anguish? Was this not betrayal? Did he not sound like an "Uncle Tom?" However, Jeremiah had a Godly perspective, not just an emotional response to the crisis.

His perspective was based on principles, the eternal principles of God's word. He knew that repeated sin and rebellion would result in destruction. By the way, un-forgiveness is a sin. He prophesied that Israel would be carried away to Babylon, and that they would remain there for a long time.

Nebuchadnezzar conquered Israel, and confusion spread among the Jews concerning the direction that Israel should take to secure its future. It was an internal war to fill the leadership vacuum left by the departed heroes. This is similar to the unspoken conflict going on between the various schools of thought about how to move forward after our history of slavery and after the gains of the civil rights and global liberation movements. The roots of both perspectives run very deep. It places brother against brother and sister against sister. Both mean well, but both can't be right. You cannot walk in two directions at the same time. The problems in our communities today are a result of wrong leadership on many levels.

In the first half of 2001 many online companies failed, because after they attracted the customers they wanted, but they had no plans to serve them. What do you do after you get what you wanted and deserve? You cannot use old clichés and old songs to deal with today's struggles. The songs of the cotton field and the sugarcane fields, civil rights movements, and even the independence struggles of the late 60s, were great melodies, but are irrelevant to lead or stir inspiration for today's struggle. We are facing many new struggles, which will require new songs, new leaders, new voices, and new strategies.

Here we are in a new millennium and charges and countercharges continue to fly. Strong arguments are raised. Defamation and name-calling is in the air. It is unfortunate that we use terms such as "race traitor", Uncle Tom, "oreo", accommodator, sellout, etc., to denigrate other people of African descent whose views are different or unpopular. After all there are no homogeneous people groups, not if we are truly free. We should not promote "group think." The familiar voices are not necessarily the right voices. Sometimes it is hard for old generals to fight new battles. Meanwhile, destiny is at stake.

Hananiah, the popular opposition to Jeremiah, gave an emotional and sentimental analysis of the dilemma the Israelites found themselves in during the captivity by Babylon. Emotional arguments are very easy to sell, but they are not always the full story. He stated that within two years Babylon's yoke would be gone. He went on to publish his views that all the treasures would be quickly returned. He toured the countryside with the proclamation that Israel's King would be back on the throne again. His message would fit well in Jamaica. He was saying, "No problem man. Every ting cris!" In fact, he went as far as to take the yoke off Jeremiah's shoulder, and breaking it before everyone in a dramatic fashion. In today's context we would say that he humiliated Jeremiah during a nationally televised debate. Can you imagine the emotions that were stirred up and the desire for liberty that was awakened? I wish Hananiah was right. But, he was not.

Life is complex, and so the simplest and cleanest answer is not always the correct solution. Think about it for a minute. If you need to learn to swim, would you just jump in the deep end? What is the goal anyway, to learn to swim or to get wet? That is the essence of the tension today. Do we want healing from the wounds of the past or temporary relief from the pressure? Godly principles promotes permanent solutions.

Jeremiah's prophecy was unpopular, but it was based on the eternal Word of God. It was backed up by Divine principles. History supported it. It was not a rosy picture; he put the time of freedom at 70 years. Why? Maybe the goal was to prepare a group of healed people with strong godly character. I know this; "It is better to trust in the Lord than to put confidence in (man's timetable)." God's solution is always better than man's.

Jeremiah said to Hananiah, "You have broken the yokes of wood, but you have made in its place yokes of iron." In fact, he went on to publicly accuse Hananiah of causing the people to trust in a lie. He claimed that Hananiah, knowingly or ignorantly, made the people's experience worse by giving them false hope, false vision, and false expectations. It was false hope because it was not based on the principles of God's word. Social solutions which violate the principles of the scriptures will not work.

Jeremiah knew that houses built on sand would not stand, regardless of how much love was in the house or the reputation of the architect. Simply because you want something to work out does not mean that it is going to work out. You might expect a certain outcome in life, but there are no guarantees that your expectation will be fulfilled. Simply saying so, does not make it so. There are many examples around us of leaders, founders and entrepreneurs who had good intentions to begin with, but who ended in devastation and destruction.

The Apostle Paul asked this question of the Galatians in chapter 3 verses 2 to 4:

> This only I want to learn from you: Did you receive the Spirit by the works of the law or by the hearing of faith? Are you so foolish? Having begun in the Spirit (that is, dealing with the problems according to the principles of the Word of God) are you being made perfect by the flesh? Have you (and I and, our ancestors) suffered so many things in vain?

Jeremiah's confrontation with Hananiah marked a critical moment in the history of the people. He had to engage Hananiah in this debate. This is a hard thing to do. It is easier to keep your views to yourself and a few friends, but Jeremiah had to obey the Word of the Lord. He said to Hananiah, "…This year you shall die, because you have taught rebellion against the Lord." Hananiah died that same year.

The irony is that Hananiah was probably given a heroes' funeral for his theories and efforts for the community, even though they did not work. The battle of the perspectives continues today. It is not good enough to be charismatic. It is no longer good enough to simply be a good orator, a good singer, deejay and crowd-mover. It is not good enough to "identify" with the people. Are you helping or hurting us? Are you bringing healing or perpetuating the pain? Where can we find healing?

There are some philosophies and concepts about the future that are prone to fail. They need to die, not next year, not ten years from now, but this very year. It is time for God's perspective to rule the day. It is not good enough to be progressive and make no progress. I believe that Jeremiah's perspective on the dilemma in Babylon speaks to the concerns among the African Diaspora today. You are a part of what is considered the African Diaspora if you can trace some measure of your heritage and history to former African slaves.

As we see in Israel's experience, a word from God is important. It may not immediately change the situation, but it will eventually change everything. Godly wisdom prepares the present to become the future. It prepares our attitude to achieve the right altitude. There would have been no need for God to say, "Let there be light" if light already existed. Darkness is an opportunity for light to shine. Present darkness is not the only possibility. Darkness is only the absence of light for now. It is not the last word on the matter. God's perspective will end the hurt that you feel. It will also end the confusion. His word will give you stability, and secure your future, and that of your children and your children's children. It will give hope for tomorrow. It will instruct you on the steps to take to align yourself to get what God is about to give. It will break the cycles of destruction. This approach will result in inner peace, an inner sense of destiny, and a foundation to build on. It will give you the right perspective.

I believe that those who understand and receive this word from God will have the "smell of the slaves ships" forever cleansed and removed from their nostrils. Let us not believe for one moment that God is on the side of confusion. He is for you. It is possible to live lives where the memories of past wrongs are not accompanied with anxiety, fear, pain, anger nor shame. God is bringing those who trust Him into wholeness and giving them the joy of fulfilling their destiny. Now is the time.

# Chapter 6

## Debating the Next Steps

The people of African descent are responsible to find ways to build a united future for all citizens.. The future of a nation belongs to everyone whether or not their fore-parents were slaves, slave owners, both or none of the above. None of us paid to be born here. We did not ask to be here. We did not request to be born into to a certain family nor to inherit a certain ethnicity. The fact that we were born during this era and are citizens in free democratic nations should mean something. So the root of the debate which we face today is about the future. What kind of future will we build in the 21$^{st}$ century?

The African diaspora is made up of the descendants of those ripped from Africa's coastline and sold throughout the western hemisphere. They are prime ministers, presidents, governors and governor generals, and chiefs of staff of armies. They are farmers, entrepreneurs, owners, laborers, educators, artists, athletes, corporate executives, presidents of universities, etc. In other words, they are just ordinary people. They are literally everywhere. They are multi-colored, multi-cultural, multi-talented, and speak a variety of languages. They have a diversity of economic and educational backgrounds and in many countries we are not the minority, but the majority.

The population of the 46 nations in South and Central America and the Caribbean stood at about 519 million at the beginning of the 21$^{st}$ Century. The population of North America, which includes USA, Canada, Bermuda, Greenland, St. Pierre is 309 million. 11.4% of the North American population are of African heritage, compared to 9.1% in Central and South America and the Caribbean. However, bear in mind that in most of the Caribbean nations, citizens with African roots make up at 85-90%

of the population. In the US 12.4%, in Cuba 62% and in Haiti 99.9% of the populations are descendants of Africans.

The first stop of slaves in the Western Hemisphere was the town of Bali, Brazil. Today 11% of Brazil's population of 209 million are of African descent, which gives them the highest concentration of people of African heritage in the Americas. William Drax visited Brazil in the 1640s, but later saw the possibility of great wealth by planting sugar cane in the English-speaking West Indies. He took a model of a sugar cane plantation with him back to Barbados. The promise of large amounts of money on the back of free, slave labor led to an unprecedented expansion of the slave trade. An arrangement, called the Atlantic Triangle, which included Europe, Africa and the Americas, was set up. It lasted for about 200 years. It is still unclear how many people left Africa to the New World, because many did not make it across the middle passage. However researchers estimated that number to be over 200 million. The struggle for healing and settlement out of this terrible experience is long overdue.

Slavery was abolished on August 1, 1838 in the English-speaking world, three years after it was officially decided. On September 22, 1862 Abraham Lincoln issued the Emancipation Proclamation in the US, but it could not be enforced until in 1865 at the end of the Civil War. Many people have made outstanding and selfless contributions to the welfare of people of African descent since then. The progress of the African diaspora is simply one of the amazing story of human history. However, in spite of the progress, we are far from healed. The scars are still tender. Many have obtained freedom and independence, but do not feel free, and yet here we are in the 21st Century!

Indeed, it seems that attitudes and expectations have gotten worse. Hopelessness, apathy and cynicism appear entrenched in our community. The Christian faith and conviction that once sustained our fore parents is no longer attractive enough for the desires and longings of their descendants of today. One of the reason for this breakdown in the transference of the faith from one generation to the next is that the Gospel requires individual, personal commitments, not political or cultural endorsements. So each generation must choose. It is easier for the next generation to choose when they see the victory of Christ in the lives of their elders. It is easier if they see results and relevance. It is easier to choose forgiveness when we hear and see our elders modelling the courage to forgive. The younger generation needs to hear more about the victories and the possibilities than the barriers. Our children need to hear the story. They need to know whether or not they should forgive people of European background for slavery. They need a clear answer.

Many leaders in the Diaspora today do not speak of the cross in the same way that their fore parents did. They do not speak of forgiveness. Many do not speak of Christ Jesus like they once did. Many of our leader have been schooled in the Babylonians ways. They speak of a generic spirituality, not Christianity. The teachings of Christ is now generalized and lumped in with watered down "faith-based or motivational" recommendations. Fear of offending others while desiring to be politically–correct and tolerant has brought us to this point. Many do not speak of the future with any clear vision. It seems that those who speak most loudly on behalf of the African diaspora have not been healed themselves from the wounds of the past. Consequently, our young men are disillusion and many are wasting away in physical, emotional and spiritual prisons.

There are many contributors to the advancement of people of African heritage. Hopefully a quick look at what has been tried will help us to discern the path we need to take into the future. It is important to compare their philosophies, and gain wisdom from their actions.

The Rev. Dr. Martin Luther King Jr. (January 15, 1929 – April 4, 1968) remains the most popular. He was a young American Baptist minister, president of the Southern Christian

Leadership Conference and the leading voice of the civil rights movement between 1954 up to his murder in Atlanta, Georgia. The SCLC was also considered the leading organization among the "Big Six" organizations involved in the civil rights movement. The others include the National Association for the Advancement of Colored People; National Urban League; Brotherhood of Sleeping Car Porters; Student Nonviolent Coordinating Committee; and Congress of Racial Equality.

Rev. Dr. King's iconic "I Have A Dream" speech during the march on Washington on August 28, 1963, reflected his perspective of a positive future.

### I have a Dream
### By Rev. Dr. Martin Luther King Jr.

I say to you today, my friends, so even though we face the difficulties of today and tomorrow, I still have a dream. It is a dream deeply rooted in the American dream.

I have a dream that one day this nation will rise up and live out the true meaning of its creed: 'We hold these truths to be self-evident: that all men are created equal.'

I have a dream that one day on the red hills of Georgia the sons of former slaves and the sons of former slave owners will be able to sit down together at the table of brotherhood. I have a dream that one day even the state of Mississippi, a state sweltering with the heat of injustice, sweltering with the heat of oppression, will be transformed into an oasis of freedom and justice.

I have a dream that my four little children will one day live in a nation where they will not be judged by the color of their skin but by the content of their character. I have a dream today.

I have a dream that one day, down in Alabama, with its vicious racists, with its governor having his lips dripping with the words of interposition and nullification; one day right there in Alabama, little black boys and black girls will be able to join hands with little white boys and white girls as sisters and brothers. I have a dream today (Hansen, Drew (2005). *The Dream: Martin Luther King Jr. and the Speech that Inspired a Nation*. HarperCollins. p. 98.).

Many believe that this speech at the Washington March was monumental in securing the passage of the Civil Rights Act of 1964 which is far more successful and transformational than many acknowledge. The marches, the demonstrations, the advocacy and the rallies paid off with major Civil Rights laws, equal access, more opportunities, open universities, increase prosperity and increased political influence. It was Judeo-Christian principles, made clear by a preacher, Rev. Dr. Martin Luther King, which awoke the conscience of the entire USA and the world. His untimely death on April 4, 1968 left the civil rights agenda in limbo, and many frozen in the twilight zone.

Today, despite the trauma of his assassination and the subsequent struggles for leadership and direction in the civil rights movement, this dream continues to resonate among the African diaspora. Various efforts are being carried out by his children and others to "keep the dream alive."

One of the earlier influential voices among the African diaspora was Booker Taliaferro Washington who lived from 1856 to 1915. He was born into slavery in Virginia. He was only 9 years old when the Civil War ended. He literally rose up from slavery and illiteracy to become a leading educator and a leader among the African diaspora in the US at the beginning of the 1900s.

His philosophy was spelt out in his address at the Cotton States Exposition in Atlanta in 1895. He believed that if the African diaspora had education, land, and money, he could have the means to improve himself. His most notable contribution was the concept of self-help, personal grooming, and the promotion of Christian morality. These principles were integrated into the Tuskegee University, which he started in 1881 specifically for people of African descent. He believed that vocational education and self-development was the key. Many ridiculed his approach and charged him of colluding with the "whites" while his brothers suffered. They demanded a more radical approach. He was called the "Great Accommodator."

He wrote the book, *Up from Slavery*. On June 24th, 1896 he received an honorary degree from Harvard University. In his acceptance speech he said, "During the next half-century and more, my race must continue passing through the severe American crucible. We are to be tested in our patience, our forbearance, our perseverance, our power to endure wrong, to withstand temptations, to economize, to acquire and use skill; in our ability to compete, to succeed in commerce, to disregard the superficial for the real, the appearance for the substance, to be great and yet small, learned and yet simple, high and yet the servant of all." I believe that his voice is still widely overlooked and unappreciated today.

William Edward Burghardt Dubois' influence and approach eventually eclipsed Washington's. Dubois was born into a well-to-do household in 1868 and attended Fisk University in the 1880s. In 1903 he wrote the book, "*The Souls of Black Folks*." He believed that "the problem of the twentieth century is the problem of the color line." He contended that more confrontation was needed, because "merely training blacks to be a permanent underclass of skilled laborers" was to surrender leadership. Unlike Booker T. Washington, he believed that a nation could not be civilized from the bottom upward. He focused on finding and leading (what he

78

called) the talented 10% - the black college graduates and intellectuals. He led the Niagara Movement into becoming a national movement of confrontation. This is still the most popular approach to dealing with the issues affecting the African Diaspora today. He organized a pivotal Pan-African conference in France in 1919 and again in 1921.

Dubois lamented the constant conflict that he encountered in seeking to lift people out of the status quo. He described it as living with two souls - two warring ideals in one dark body. He stated that the root of the problem in our community was a conflict between being black and being American. He faced frustrations from both sides; "If we organize separately for anything: Jim Crow. If we organize with white people: Traitor. If unable to get the whole loaf we seize half to ward off starvation: Compromise. If we let the other half go and starve: Why don't you do something? Where in heavens name do we Negroes stand?" He was eventually labeled a "radical" and died in self-imposed exile in Accra, Ghana on August 27, 1963. He had become a Ghanaian citizen and an official member of the Communist Party.

Another individual in the Western Hemisphere who was well known for his struggle to help the African diaspora was Marcus Garvey. He was born in the parish of St. Ann, Jamaica on August 17, 1887. He is one of the National Heroes of Jamaica. He passionately believed that "Africa was for Africans." He rose to champion the cause of the African Diaspora worldwide. He left Jamaica and traveled across North, Central and South America. The plight of people of African diaspora in these nations prompted him to ask, "Where is the black man's government? Where are his King and his kingdom, his army and navy? I will help to make them." and he worked at it. He was a bold separationist.

He founded the United Negro Improvement Association and started several businesses. It is reported that at its peak there were some 4 million members in his organization and 1100 chapters in over 40 Countries. He was an avowed pan-Africanist and is considered the Father of contemporary Black Nationalism and Black power movement. The Rastafarian movement also claim Marcus Garvey as their prophet. The most notable of his efforts was the ill-fated Black Star Line shipping enterprise, which focused on, among other things, taking the African diaspora back to Africa. The effort failed.

The Black Star Liner did not show up, and many were left stranded and disillusioned on the Kingston harbor with their belongings stuffed into their suitcases. They believed that their healing and future was best fulfilled back in Africa. Today a group of Rastafarians in Bull Bay, Jamaica, live in their own compound called the Black Ethiopian International Congress. They claim that it is an independent country. They are still waiting for the ships to take them back to Africa. Away from Babylon (Jamaica).

Marcus Garvey was imprisoned in the USA and deported to Jamaica in December 1927. In 1935 Garvey left for England where he died in near obscurity in a cottage in West Kensington on June 10, 1940. He moved the agenda along. He brought a sense of pride and highlighted the need to think big, but healing was not found.

Growing up in Jamaica in the 1970s meant that I was fully exposed to the worldwide movement to raise the lot of people of African diaspora. Bob Marley was an evangelist and promoter for the Rastafarianism. His musical chants gave the desires a poetic voice. He grew up in the ghettoes of Kingston, Jamaica, and understood the hopelessness of the time. He was mixed race and felt the pressure from all sides. His songs of liberation and calls to "tread down Babylon" resounded among oppressed people from the Caribbean to Africa to Europe to North, Central, and South America, and even in Asia. He became very wealthy and gained worldwide fame.

He was able to rise out of the "jungle" by exercising his gift. Today his sons and grandchildren can sing about coming out of the ghetto. He is a good example of independence and persistence, but the problems and issues about which he sang persist, and have actually gotten worse. His remedy was wrong. His songs did not bring healing. Getting high and grooving to the beat was, and is, nothing more than a form of escapism. Those who followed the path he embraced remain overwhelmed. Interestingly, it is widely reported that Bob Marley was baptized into the Christian faith on his death bed.

The Rastafarian movement started in Jamaica in the 1930s. However, Marley became its most popular and outspoken propagator. Although it is not a viable option or a much-publicized objective, except for a marginalized few like the Bobo Ashanti Rastas in the hills of Bull Bay, St. Thomas, they made repatriation to Africa a strong plank in their platform. The Rastafarians took a lot of motivation from the "prophecies" of Marcus Garvey that a King would rise out of Africa to liberate the African diaspora. They embraced Haile Selassie, the former emperor of Ethiopia, as that king. He was viewed as the black alternative to a "white" Jesus who would liberate the people and "mashdown Babylon." Jamaica and the entire western hemisphere was labeled Babylon. Christianity and the western lifestyle was said to be the root of the problem.

It is important to also note that Haile Selassie did not agree with them. He was never a Rastafarian. In fact, it is reported that he sent missionaries from the Ethiopian Orthodox Church to Jamaica to teach about the ways of the One True God - and His Son Jesus Christ. Except for the popularity and money gained through reggae music, Rastafarianism exacerbated the hurt. They have not brought healing. It is so sad to see old men with long grey dreadlocks and grey bushy beards still hooked on ganja, and grooving to the beat, searching for peace.

The Rastafarian teachings and lifestyles led to the loss of millions of fine leaders – men and women. They were gifted by God to make a difference for their generation, and their descendants. The marijuana (ganja), the narcotic sacrament of Rastafarianism, turned out to be just another mood altering drug that clouds the minds, dulls the senses, and steals the potential of many young people. The music and drugs only delayed the pain. It never brought healing. Music cannot heal. It was a delusion that led to deadly addictions. So many have died along the way.

The music seduced many from the church. It gave them a broken crutch and a false sense of escape and freedom. Many are still hypnotized by the reggae beat today well into their old age in their search for healing of the soul. I hope we have not become so intoxicated with the money, the fame and the notoriety from the reggae brand that we refuse to examine its real impact on our lives.

History will not hold Rastafarianism in high regard. No objective researcher will. I believe that the "I man is god" message of Rastafarianism gave rise to the rebellious, authority hating, "self-centered" and self-rewarding focus of hip-hop and dance hall music. Rastafarianism paved the way for the culture we have today. It will not be excused from its responsibility for the many lives ruined by its teachings from the Caribbean to Africa to Europe and back. How would you deal with a doctor who was able to identify the symptoms of the problem only to give you what turned out to be a fatal prescription? Do you just ignore the results and praise his good intentions? No, they should be held accountable and others should be warned.

Haiti was the first nation in the new world to throw off the bonds of slavery. Toussaint L'Overture led a series of uprisings that virtually exterminated every European on the Island. It has been over two centuries now since the Haitian independence and yet the kind of atmosphere needed for the proper spiritual and personal development of its people remain elusive. Things are changing, though. Christians have declared Haiti as God's country and are acting like it. For the first time, they are taking ownership of the land and are rebuilding the character of the nation from inside. Watch for the desire of this people to come forth. A new approach is taking hold.

The daze from the deaths of John F. Kennedy and Martin Luther King in the 1960s is still fresh in many peoples mind. The bullets remain lodged in the hope and expectations of many. The gap in leadership continues. We hear the words of his dream. Yet when we consider how he died, what the leaders around us are saying, and we see the unresolved issues, we ask where we are today? Some are waiting for the next shoe to drop.

The search is still on for a leader for the African diaspora. But do we really need that same type of leader now? There is a major debate raging about the path forward, because it is obvious to all that in spite of the major gains and remarkable contributions things are very unsettled. In fact, I believe that a lot of young people are still torn between listening to MLK or the young Malcolm X. I say the young Malcom X, because the older and wiser Malcom X was a lot less angry than the younger.

Eleven o'clock on Sunday morning is still a segregated time in the USA and many other countries, and it seems that God's people (on all sides) love to have it so. The church - preachers - must once again take the lead to bring healing, closure, and declare the NOW Word of God; otherwise another generation will continue in the cycle of pain, disillusionment, and remain an open prey to the enemy of their soul.

In many cities with a large population of African diaspora, freedom and independence seems to have led to more confusion, selfishness, destruction, and anarchy. Some of the elderly have even expressed doubt about the wisdom of breaking away from colonial rule! Violence, fear, and hopelessness co-exist with beautiful cars, lights, money, and "progress." The younger generation is torn. Many feel disillusioned and consequently are disengage from the civic and political life of the nation of their birth. The older generation did not get them back to Africa, and many have no idea how to connect with the very nation where they are living. They are suspicious of the nation of their birth.

The issues of discrimination, racial injustices, etc. continue to cause restlessness. The fathers feel stuck in the west, where they feel unwanted and unappreciated, but cut off, unable to relate to Africa. They like the prosperity and personal freedom of the West. What to do? Many of the older generation are not healed. Their perspectives are warped by years of hurts and offenses. Consequently, they are multiplying and passing on their wounds to their descendants. The deep wounds of the past are now festering and crying for attention. The fatherless children tell the story. The mushrooming gangs tell the story. Is there no healer in sight?

The rappers are taking the cash and gleefully continuing the rap. Their success did not ease the pain. Many wonder if it is even in their capacity or interest to bring healing. It is a decision they will have to make. Their entire business plan seems to be built on exploiting the pain. The music industry is like a multi-million dollars drug ring. The patients can't get enough of it. The artistes know this and are glad to oblige and run to the bank with the spoils. The truth is that they really can't bring healing to the very pain that they are so familiar with. They can sing about it.

The movement called "Black Lives Matters" has made a stand on social justice, reparation and the reshaping of America as they desire it to be. They are concern about the unsettled issues going all the way back to the days of slavery in America. Lost in the discussion though is the value of the lives of the many people who died in the America Civil War under the American flag. The leaders of that day believed that the millions who perished was the judgement of God on America for the sin of slavery. They believe that the millions who died shed their blood for a reason.

The tension between police and our young black men is not limited to America. There is a serious standoff, distrust and disconnect between law enforcement and the African diaspora, especially young men, in most countries in the western hemisphere. I lay responsibility for this tension at the feet of the culture fostered by the reggae, hip hop and dancehall artistes as well as educators and other social engineers. We can change the way the Police approach us, by changing the way we approach the police and the way we present ourselves.

Some who are more contemplative have turned to various Eastern and African customs. Hip hop is even developing its own spirituality and cult fetish. Many have ignored Christianity and have adopted different forms of ancestral worship in a bid to find a sense of identity and connection somewhere. Kwanzaa is an example of this search. The Nation of Islam does not have the Word that heals. The Hebrew Israelite movement is an example of our search for meaning.

A fellow preacher from Ghana gave me a glimpse into the going back to Africa movement. He informed me that every year thousands from among the diaspora make an annual pilgrimage to Accra, Ghana, to celebrate and connect with the past. Many of the people in the Caribbean have Ghanaian roots. The Ghanaian established a national tourism board to welcome these "lost brethren" back home and lead them in all kinds of "ceremonial cleansing and rituals" to wash away the evil experiences of their ancestors and the passage of time. This is all in a bid to find healing and inner peace.

To the unsuspecting individual from the African diaspora, this is a highly significant or even spiritual way of dealing with the past, but for many Ghanaians it is about the money. It is just another tourist trap. It makes a mockery of the deep need for closure that the African diaspora seeks.

The terrible design of the devil was also exposed when he told me that ordinary Ghanaians would never do those ceremonies. Ghanaian Christians would not perform them, because those ceremonies were considered as "spiritual pacts." My friend from Ghana asked me to warn my brethren in the Caribbean to be careful about these tricks. Substitutes for healing are only temporary delusions. Let me hasten to say that there is nothing wrong with re-connecting with the people of Africa, because there are many noble things and many contributions for our lives there today. But how? Where? With whom?

We must also clarify a few pieces of misinformation about Africa. There is no "pure African" culture. Well, let me say, that there are no "pure cultures" anywhere in the world. Everyone is influenced by someone. Sin, and error knows no borders, boundaries, color nor language. The continent of Africa consists of over 58 different nations and over 784 million people with over 2110 distinct languages groups. We must get rid of the naive and paternalistic view of Africa. Africa is made of a variety of nations, a diversity of cultures, many tribes and languages, and many rich and important concepts.

The recent advances in DNA studies is putting the entire race discussion on its head. The science is proving what the Bible said all along. We're all from one blood, and more over people are finding out that they are mixed up with some of the people that offended them and might have oppressed their fore parents. What should I do if my great-great grandfather was the slave master of my wife's great-great grandmother? The cultural purity or racial purity argument cannot be taken seriously in the 21st century. The way forward is not racial segregation. That will not bring healing. It only promotes isolation, insulation, and bitterness.

Several people from Jamaica and the Caribbean who pulled up roots and moved to Ethiopia in the 1970s have found out that it is not as simple as it sounds. Others, such as the late Bob Marley's wife, Rita, and several Jamaicans were given land in some countries so that they could settle in and make a new home.

There are many people who believe that the problems of prejudice and discrimination do not exist in the Caribbean or in South and Central America. And, though it might be tempting to say, "Oh, we have no problem, mon", that would be far from the truth. The same problems exist among people with differing hues and shades of black skin. Various caste systems exist, and, yes, race matters remain an issue by those seeking political offices to stir emotions and move the votes in their favor. Many suffer hurt, discrimination and offenses at the hands of their own relatives.

The Bible does not elevate cultures nor race above others; it teaches Godly operating principles and those who follow them prosper and are elevated. God did not endorse the culture of Israel simply because they were Jews. God chose to reveal His love to the world through the Jewish people, not because of their culture, but in-spite of it. Their culture and uniqueness is tied to what God made them to be as they obeyed and follow Him. Abraham believed God and that "was counted for righteousness" and then God made a covenant with him. He was endorsed and blessed for his obedience.

Culture is defined as the accepted norms or ways of living of a group of people. Culture is therefore learned. No one is born with a cultural DNA stamp. Our culture is made up of decisions that have become acceptable or tolerable to us over time. After a while, these repeated decisions form habits. These habits become the accepted response or norms and the results become the expected outcome. But it all started somewhere. There is a philosophy or reason behind every decision. Every action is guided by a Godly principle or the lack thereof.

If you trace the history of Europe, you will find that at some point in their history, there was a willingness to search out and translate Biblical principles for personal development, personal prosperity and nation building into actual laws and institutions. Over time the European society became increasingly influenced by the principles found in the Bible. Its teaching moved them from serfdom and feuding tribes into civilized co-existence. The Bible was the textbook for the lawyers, judges and politicians. The abolition of slavery was obtained because the abolitionists used the compass of the word of God to inform men's consciences. The God-given rights of people – slaves, servants, children, women, the sick, the educational rights, the concept of freedom and democracy, individual ownership and rights – are all principles that helped to develop Europe. As Europe ignores God and removes the moral command of the Bible from its social and political life, the more regressive they've become.

Today, you'll find that the nations with the best environment for the proper development of their people are those who apply the Biblical principles for personal development, personal prosperity and nation-building. The Bible is for freedom. It supports individual pursuit of destiny. It works. I believe we need to look at the Bible again and find the principles for personal growth and community development. Healing is found in Jesus, not in government initiatives.

You cannot go forward by making backward decisions. The principles for good governance and individual destiny are secured and revealed in the Scriptures. The very concept of education and the rationale for universities for ordinary people were inspired by the Word of God. These advances in society were not made because the people are somehow "better." It's not the people. It's the principles. People are people everywhere. It is the belief systems and behavior of people that make the difference between societies.

Following God's principles brought the African diaspora a long way, yet the debate rages. Why change partners now? Where were the politically correct social commentators when our fore parents were in the fields trying to survive? Where were the atheists then? Where were those who would now want to hijack the civil right movement for their lifestyle choices? How can anyone compare their choice of behavior to the involuntary color of one's skin? Isn't that a sign of disrespect, abuse and disregard for the history of pain of the African diaspora?

The abolitionists did not stand on the secular opinion of the majority. In fact if secularism had prevail over Biblical morality in government and Supreme Court of old, slavery would still be a celebrated and legal commercial system. The abortionist stood on the Bible. Why stop now? Why have we not wholeheartedly embrace Godly principles in order to deal with the present and define the future? Let's go all the way. Are we so consumed with peoples' attitudes towards our skin color that we have ignored our responsibility to develop our own character? Our Godly character was the one golden quality which Rev. Dr. Martin Luther King Jr dreamt about. We need to get back our godly character.

When the apostle Paul encouraged believers to pray for the government and civic leaders, he revealed that the Godly function of these offices was to preserve and safeguard the atmosphere for citizens to dream and pursue those dreams with minimum hindrances.

> *"Therefore, I exhort first of all that supplication, prayers, intercessions, and giving of thanks be made for all men, for kings and all who are in authority, that we may lead a quiet and peaceable life in all godliness and dignity."*
> (1 Timothy 2:1-2)

> *"Therefore you are inexcusable, O Man...But we know that the judgment of God is according to truth... for there is no partiality with God."* (From Romans 2: 1, 2 &11)

> *"The just shall live by faith."* (Hebrews 10:38)

Note that the motivation to apply all manner of prayers "for kings and all who are in authority" was so that the citizens could live a prosperous and dignified life informed by their faith in God. That is the purpose of all governments.

Many who sacrificed much in the marches, strikes and fights for our civil rights, and independence are disillusioned and frustrated. This frustration can be summed up by the remarks of the ex-wife of a former Jamaican Prime Minister after the brutal killing of a matriarch of Jamaica's' fight for independence. She lamented, "What was all the marching and singing and demonstration for…" I also met an old Buffalo Soldier motivational speaker from Houston, Texas who asked the same question. The anguish was vivid in his voice as he wondered what was happening to his people. He wondered why African Americans were turning away from the very God that sustained them in the fight for freedom. The cry of confusion, disillusionment, desperation, and fear is everywhere.

The following statements reflects the feeling of many in the African diaspora in the Caribbean, as well as North, Central and South America: "I can't go back to Africa. My country is not working. I will never be accepted here. The harder I try, the more the barriers seem to go up. The more I try to be accepted, the more somebody hurts me. I try to reach across the aisle and break out of my neighborhood, my family laughs at me and mocks my progress. Who am I? I feel caged? Will I ever live outside of this box?"

The past wounds are very deep; the confusion is debilitating, and the future remains bleak. Many of our young men simply do not think about the future, it is too painful and uncertain. Many conclude that they will live a very short life. They simply do whatever is needed to get by for today. It is survival time. They are willing to do anything to get rich quick. It's all about the grind. The guiding philosophy is YOLO (You Only Live Once), so get all you can as fast as you can.

This internal agony, deception and sense of hopelessness cannot be ignored by any caring person. Political, security, educational and social development plans will not succeed if these factors continue to be ignored.

There are many other important contributors - positive and negative - to the journey of the African diaspora who were not highlighted in this book. They have all brought us to this day. The Civil Rights leaders of yesteryear in the USA did well, but the fight is different now. The independence fighters did well. But we need new strategies.

It is time to return to the God who brought us out of bondage and to renew those strategies that work. We need wisdom. We need prophetic voices to declare the NOW word of God. It is time for a new perspective and a new approach. It is not too late to experience God's will. We have already lost a lot of ground, but if this generation hears, receives, and applies the Word of God we can break the cycle. We don't have to accept the status quo. I believe that Jeremiah's perspective is here.

## "You Have What it Takes"
### by
### George Washington Carver

Figure it out for yourself, my lad
You have all that the greatest of men have had
Two legs, two hands, two eyes
And a brain to use if you be wise.
With this equipment that all began
So get hold of yourself and say "I can."

Look them over, the wise and the great
They take their food from a common plate.
Similar knife and forks they use,
And with similar laces they ties their shoes,
But the world considers them brave and smart
But you have all they had when they made their start.

You can triumph and come to skill
You can be great if only you will.
You have two legs, two hands, two eyes,
And a brain to use if you be wise.
But courage must come from the soul within.
A man must furnish that will to win!

So figure it out for yourself, my lad;
You have all that the greatest of men have had.
Two legs, two hands, two eyes –
And a brain to use if you be wise.
With this equipment that all began,
So get hold of yourself and say, "I can!"

## Chapter 7

## Coming Full Circle

The scripture is abundantly clear about God's commitment to move oppressed people into liberty. "Where the Spirit of the lord is, there is liberty" (2 Corinthians 3:17b). The birth of Jesus Christ was accompanied by a host of angels announcing, "Glory to God in the highest and on earth, peace and Good Will to ALL men." The very essence of Christianity is the gospel is – good news. Christ has been referred to as the Lord, the liberator and the redeemer throughout human history.

In Hebrews 12 verse 28 the scriptures shows that Christianity ushers in a kingdom or realm of living where freedom and liberty is not just spiritual, it is practical. Spiritual, political and personal freedom are core principles of Christianity. The scripture also states that where the Spirit of the Lord is not quenched, but allowed to reveal and lead people into the will of God, the end result will be freedom for all. However, freedom is gift. It is an invitation into a certain kind of lifestyle. It is a value system that must be personally accepted and entered into. It is a way of life, not a legislative award. True freedom comes only from God. It starts within and works itself outward into every area of society.

Jeremiah's prophetic word to Israel, written in Jeremiah chapter 29, is relevant to us today. It is God's perspective concerning the history of oppressed people everywhere. Read it and see if you can identify your situation in it:

*Thus says the Lord of hosts, the God of Israel, to all who were carried away captive, whom I have caused to be carried away from Jerusalem to Babylon:*

*Build houses and dwell in them; plant gardens and eat their fruit. Take wives and beget sons and daughters; and take wives for your sons and give your daughters to husbands, so that they may bear sons and daughters*
*— that you may be increased there, and not diminished.*
*And seek the peace of the city where I have caused you to be carried away captive, and pray to the Lord for it; for in its peace you will have peace. (Emphasis mine.)*
*For I know the thoughts that I think toward you, says the Lord, thoughts of peace and not of evil,*
*to give you a future and a hope.*

*Then you will call upon Me and go and pray to Me, and I will listen to you.*
*And you will seek Me and find Me, when you search for Me with all your heart.*
*I will be found by you, says the Lord, and I will bring you back from your captivity;*
*I will gather you from all the nations and from all the places where I have driven you, says the Lord,*
*and I will bring you to the place from which I cause you to be carried away captive* (Jeremiah 29:4-14).

If you should embrace these truths as your worldview they will lead you into a Godly perspective of life. As Jesus used the scriptures to overcome His trials so must you. When Jesus was faced with His enemies He responded from a Godly perspective, and so should you. Jesus' basic reaction to offenses was to follow the instructions of the Word of God. You can sum up the Jesus way of living in this one statement which He made at the beginning of His ministry, "Man shall not live by bread alone, but by every word that proceeds out of the mouth of God."

So here are some specific instructions for you from this Jeremiah prophecy:

## 1. "Build houses and dwell in them"

In other word, possess the land. You should develop a landowner mentality. Think and plan for the long term. It is a risk worth taking. It is an encouragement for us to prepare for more than just this month's bills and expenses, but set a foundation of prosperity for your children's children. You will be here for a long time; you're not going anywhere soon. Your fore parents were brought here against their will, but you were born here by the will of God. It is no accident that you were born here. You could have been born anywhere in the world during any period of human history, but God sent you here now. You belong here.

I know that the Messiah will return, but do what he said; "occupy till I come" (Luke 19:13). So settle down. Buy real estate instead of renting all the time. We should insist that our governments system make landownership easy. It is time to go beyond simply living and working to pay the bills, eat, buy more stuff, get more entertainment and sleep somewhere to get up and do it again year after year. Don't give away your hard earned money to the corporations and artistes who hire smart advertisers to hook consumers. Why would you call your house a crib? Are you a baby? Words matter. A crib is a temporary place that someone else is responsible to take care of and prepare for us. If your house is a crib you are denying your personal responsibility for your future. God has a higher purpose for your life.

## 2. "Plant gardens and eat their fruit."

God is encouraging you to invest your money. Let your hard earn money work for you. Invest in the stock markets, help someone to start a new business or become an investors in a company that is already existing. In spite of the "crashes" in the stock markets across the world, there is a lot of opportunity to prosper on Wall Street and in the stock markets of nations around the world with smaller economies. Wall Street is not the only place to invest! Check out the opportunities in the nations of Africa.

You may have to start your own businesses -be an entrepreneur. Give your children and grandchildren investment accounts instead of more "stuff" for their Christmas and birthdays. Notice that the instruction is to plant gardens – create opportunities for residual income. To plant gardens, also mean to go back to the farms where your fore parents were slaves and work them now for yourself. The wealth is in the ground. Just because your fore parents did not get paid for their farming does not mean farming is bad. Farming is where the wealth is. Everything depended on the ground. You honor the legacy of your fore parents when you farm. Go for it.

### 3. "Take wives and beget sons."

It's time to make marriage special again. So get married instead of settling for the insecure and temporary status as a fiancé, girlfriend or boyfriend. God wants you to get married and start a family. Statistics affirms what the Bible teaches. Children do better in their personal development and in life if they are raised in a home where father and mother are married. Children should be birthed within the security of a married home. Children in single parent homes have a greater risk for poverty and also for developing unhealthy behaviors. It is not too late to start.

We should encourage marriage. If you are willing to live with someone, sleep with them, take care of them, have their children, then you should marry them? We need more sons, because sons will become fathers. They will extend the generations to come. As the fathers go, so goes the family and society.

Only in the days of slavery did a man have a child and leave it for someone else, e.g. the government, to take care of. If you're still doing that, then you are stuck in the wrong era. In the past, men were used as breeding studs, but those days are over. You have 100% of the responsibility to provide for ALL of your children.

## 4. "Give your sons and daughters in marriage"

We must teach our children that marriage is the only acceptable adult lifestyle. So prepare them for marriage. Promote marriage. We should honor and defend marriage as a scared and exclusive union between one man and one woman. Let's champion the case of children and the unborn. Descendant of African slaves should form the most strident opposition to abortion, and to same sex "marriage."

One of the blessing of giving our sons and daughters in marriage is that you will not always be a minority in the land. One of God's blessing on your life is to give you children. We reject the blessing of more children because we ourselves are not healed. We allow people from all over the world to migrate into our homelands and raise their children to reap the benefits, while we are sidelined by our hurt and our pain. We stopped marrying and having children. We stopped believing in the future. Today, instead of planning our families God's way, we have embraced secular family planning methods. Many of these family planning methods were developed by people who did not have the best interest of the people of African heritage at heart. If you stop marrying and having children in the institution of marriage you will surrender your land and wealth to others. You have trashed any hope of redemption of all the hard work and suffering of your forefathers.

## 5. "Seek the peace of the city where you are living."

God wants you to accept responsibility for your community. You have the right and the ability to set the atmosphere of the town or city where you are living. You have that right even if you are a newcomer and have no historical ties. The fact is that if you were born in that country then it is your city or your country, you now have historical ties to it! It's your birthright. Say it out loud, "This is my City."

Seek the peace of the city. Look for it, find ways to increase peace among the people. There will be no peace in our cities until we accept that the citizens and residents in the city are more responsible for the quality life in the city than the politicians and law enforcement agents.

Do something to help in its improvement and development. You have something to contribute. Get involved. Vote. Get involved in the local civic groups. Join the school board. Form a neighborhood watch. Call crime stop or the FBI and report those who are perpetuating crimes, forming gangs, holding the neighborhood hostage and practicing extortion of the business owners. You can develop the character of your city. You do it. Don't wait for preachers, politicians, or policemen or a more "qualified" person. Stop cursing the dark. Turn on your light. If you see the need, then tag, you're it!

Note that the Bible says to seek the peace. Therefore, you'll have to be persistent and committed to the result of peace.

### 6. "Pray for the peace of the city, for in its peace you will have peace."

It is amazing what collaboration will do for you and for the entire city. It is time to go across the tracks and connect with people of like mind to form civic groups, neighborhood prayer groups to pray for the City and organize churches to worship together. There will be a great revival when people of different racial and ethnic groups get together to focus on the need of the City. In other words, it is not about us, but about our town, our neighborhood, our city and our nation.

It's about our families. It is important that you see your future tied to the success of everyone in your city. Own it. Act like you belong. Clean up the neighborhood. Success is not necessarily moving up town! The Dr. Martin Luther King Boulevards across America should be the best kept, most neighborly and safest place in the entire City. You should see yourself as a stakeholder in your city.

Let's make our neighborhoods and towns a place where our children and young people have a sense of belonging and connection. It should be a place where they feel safe and accepted. Make it a place where they can grow and live happy lives. It is not too late. It is not impossible. Lets' pray for the peace of our cities.

## 7. "Do not let your prophets and your diviners deceive you."

It is possible to be deceived even if our intentions are completely noble and godly. Just because someone is a prophet, or because at one time they exhibited some spiritual influence over your life, does not mean that what they are teaching at the present time is the truth. In order for you to begin living your life with this new perspective you will need to study the Word of God for yourself. You need the truth. You need to develop discernment. Do not give in to sentimental and emotional reactions. Try the spirit. Check the motive.

You can discern the truthfulness of anyone by praying for wisdom, comparing what they say with the Bible and examining the fruits of their lives. Are they living a holy Christ-like life? The fruits of the Spirit should be evident in the life of any true prophet: love, joy, peace, longsuffering, kindness, goodness, faithfulness, gentleness, self-control (Galatians 5:22).

## 8. "I will cause you to return."

God will cause you to return. He has promised you victory. Trust His timetable and His agenda. God has a future for you. So give Him the controls and allow Him to make the future what it should be. He will settle it all. To "return" shows a sense of fulfillment or of coming full circle. Your history will one day make sense to you. You will find your purpose. Sometimes our dreams and longings for "yesteryear" can hurt our today and cloud our tomorrows. Keep your eyes on the Lord and He will bring you full circle. It will all make sense to you. You will feel fulfilled. If you walk with God, you will arrive at your destination.

**9. "For I know the thoughts that [I have always had] towards you, says the Lord, thoughts of peace and not of evil to give you a future and a hope."**

God has a mind of His own! He is very creative. His thoughts about you are more than the sands on the seashore. He has been thinking about you a lot. Now get it right. He is not thinking how to judge you, hurt you, punish you or some negative thing about you. He is telling you the nature of His thoughts about you. The question is whether you believe Him or not?

He has been keeping His eyes on you. Allow Him to free you internally- spiritually and mentally - even as He has freed you politically. He wants to bless you beyond your wildest dream. Don't stop now. Keep growing. Keep changing. Keep learning. Your history does not diminish His thoughts towards you. The fact that you and your fore parents have suffered injustices and prejudices does not change His will for your life. God's thoughts about you are not shaped by the opinions of others. Whose opinion are you allowing to shape your future?

Who imagined that you or others like you and me would have been so blessed and so free? The best is yet to come. I know there is a lot of talk of the end of the world. I don't know, but I do know that God did not instruct us to order some "meals-to-go" and climb under a rock somewhere to wait to die. God has a plan for our lives. You have a Destiny. Discover it. Develop it. Become it. God is waiting on you.

This message from Jeremiah is full of hope. There is no doom and gloom here even though he delivered it while Israel was in Babylon. This reflects the very nature of God. This is the right perspective on our history. This passage in Jeremiah 29 offers hope to the Tutsi and the Hutus in the Congo, Shiites and the Sunnis in Iraq, as well as the Arabs and Jews the Middle East. It offers healing to "black" and "white." It brings hope for change to those caught in today's shadowy slave trades. It offers hope to those wrongly imprisoned across the world. God is impartial. He is forever against anything that hinders men from fulfilling their destiny.

That is why Christians are encouraged to pray for those in authority. We need an atmosphere of impartiality and freedom to pursue our God-given potential. God is for democracy. Men are even free to rebel against Him. Dictatorships, government control and strong arm tactics are anti-Biblical.

You might think that it is easy to have this positive perspective when everything is going well at home. But remember that Israel was occupied by Babylon when this prophecy was given. Its best and brightest were taken away. The Babylonians were carrying out a sophisticated brainwashing strategy. Many leaders were sidelined, blacklisted and imprisoned. The temples were destroyed. Their community halls were knocked to the ground. Businesses were stolen and shut down. The young women were being abused. The crime rate was off the charts. Israel was being plundered. It was a time of great confusion; no one knew the way forward. It was in that environment that God reminded them that He was still thinking about them. It was in that mess that He came up with a creative solution for the challenges which they faced.

The approach by God to the various ebbs and flows of human history is consistent. He does not need an ideal situation to initiate His plan. You do not need to be the "BMIT" (Big Man In Town) to fulfill the dreams which God placed in your heart. He is thinking about your victory. He is developing a plan for your advantage.

The word of God will not return void. God does not run away from darkness, pain or the problems of the day. Chaos and confusion do not faze Him. It is our attempt to use the knowledge of good and evil instead of faith in Him that is the biggest hindrance. To react in isolation to Godly wisdom will only increase the darkness and delay the light.

Although a prisoner in Roman jail, the apostle Paul asked the following rhetorical questions:

What shall we then say to these things? If God be for us, who can be against us? He that spared not his own Son, but delivered him up for us all, how shall he not with him also freely give us all things? Who shall lay anything to the charge of God's elect?...Who is he that condemneth? ...Who shall separate us from the love of Christ?

Shall tribulation, or distress, or persecution, or famine, or nakedness, or peril, or sword? As it is written, For thy sake we are killed all the day long; we are accounted as sheep for the slaughter.

Nay, in all these things we are more than conquerors through him that loved us. For I am persuaded, that neither death, nor life, nor angels, nor principalities, nor powers, nor things present, nor things to come, nor height, nor depth, nor any other creature, shall be able to separate us from the love of God, which is in Christ Jesus our Lord (Romans 8:31-39 KJV).

We could add to this list such things like broken families; Sons in jail; Abortions; Corruption; Guns; Drugs; Prostitution; Modernization; Riches; 10 Benz and three houses; illiteracy; Many empty Churches; Prejudice; Discrimination; Joblessness; wars; globalization, etc. and the answer will still be the same: we shall overcome. *"Yet in all these things we are more than conquerors through Him who loved us" (verse 37).*

You don't need a perfect situation to be successful in life. You just need to be confident that God has a perfect plan you're your future and follow Him into it. The word confidence simply means to act with faith in the truth.

Some of the most successful people in life faced the most daunting of obstacles. Joseph was sold into slavery by his brothers and yet prospered in Egypt. Daniel and the Hebrew boys fulfilled their destiny in life under Babylonian captivity. In Genesis 1:1, the Spirit of the Lord moved upon the face of the deep when the earth was without order, chaotic and unproductive, absent of anything good. However, God spoke into that chaos and said, "Let there be LIGHT!" And miracle of miracles, "THERE WAS LIGHT."

When God gives an order, and the Holy Spirit is not hindered, light will come. Positive change will happen. God is speaking today. Choose to let the light shine in your hearts, in your homes and in your communities. This light will dispel the dark memories of the past.

The prophet Jeremiah was defining the worldview or perspective of followers of Jesus Christ. The source of a Christian's present and future success is Jesus, the blessings of Abraham and the revealed Word of God. The government is not and should never be considered as the source, God is. Therefore, regardless of the situation in which they were born or the kind of "life" they were "handed" they knew that God had a formula for success. This should be our approach today.

The Bible says, "Where no oxen are, the trough is clean: but much increase is by the strength of the ox" (Proverbs 14:4). There will always be some mess around somewhere when you are active. "Stuff" will happen when you're working. The solution is not to stop working because things are getting messy and smelly. You cannot wait until everything is perfect to step forward.

Solomon rightly calls the man who will not leave his house, because there is a lion in the way, a slothful man. God puts a fire for success in your belly for you to follow. Don't wait for all the issues to be settled to your complete satisfaction before you start your journey towards healing. Start now!

There will never be total consensus for your success! Total agreement does not even happen in our families, much less in a entire nation of different ethnic groups. People are people and they have their own minds. I encourage you to accept God's perspective and get a better view of your past, get a picture of the future that God has for you, embrace the promise of that future and start working it.

I remember the fear that came over me when I felt that God wanted me to be a preacher. I was so afraid. I thought that He would surely kill me or strike me with some awful disease if I didn't do it. Then I was afraid that He would simply make my life completely miserable if I did. I really thought that serving God was like getting a life imprisonment inside a church building, with an old saint playing an out of tune organ.

Today, after many years of following Jesus, I can testify that my life is what I secretly wanted it to be. God knew what was in my heart even before I understood it. My end is secure. It is in Him. I've come full circle. I would not hesitate to encourage anyone to pursue Gods' perfect will for their life, especially if it is to be a preacher like me! He sees our end, and then we must allow Him to teach us how to get there. It is God who gives you the power to get wealth so that He might establish His covenant (Deuteronomy 8:18).

Government exists for some things; however, there are many things, which could be hindered by government and legislative actions. I encourage you to turn away from putting your future in government systems or in the efforts of men. Trust in God. The best way forward is to live your life, raise your children and make your plans in accordance with the principles of God's word and the spirit of Christ instead of political maneuverings, the latest psychological publications or polling data. If you live by faith your prayers will be answered and many things that are outstanding will come to pass. The churches will be full again. The testimonies will flow again and miracles will be plenty again.

God is very much in control and ready to bring in the re-enforcement, but He cannot support a wrong agenda and a wrong perspective. God may seem to be late, but He is always on time. I believe that as we enter into this new millennium, we will see the story of our history, and life experiences come full circle, and the devil's blatant exploitation of God's children will be pushed back on every front. The enemy is in retreat.

I submit that soon thousands of Christians of African heritage will make a reverse trek across the Atlantic Ocean. In fact many are doing that today. Many groups such as Youth With A Mission and others have retraced the Atlantic Triangle – Europe to Africa to the Americas/Caribbean –with the gospel. These groups acted in representation of the entire African diaspora as they stopped at each port connected to the slave trade. They prayed. They repented. They heard the repentance of the descendants of slave catchers, slave merchants and slave-owners living in Africa and Europe. They forgave. They blessed others. It is awesome what is happening.

I believe that millions more from the African diaspora will go to Europe and to Africa to declare, "Look what the Lord has done. We have come full circle, and it is all because of the grace of the Lord God of heaven. We love all and forgive all."

I believe that this will ignite massive changes in many nations across Africa and the world. The testimony of God's grace will send ripple effects around the world. A new era will be ushered in across the continent of Africa when healing comes. The world will see the example of our walk of forgiveness, and harmony and learn again from the African diaspora. A new sense of harmony and brotherhood will be birthed in the earth. A bold message of healing and faith in Jesus Christ will be preached. A principled stand on the Word of God on such issues as the equality of all will follow.

There will be a strong emphasis for everyone globally to prosper, have civil rights, freedom and democracy and access to the gospel. Many leaders across the globe are still ignoring the Godly principles of freedom and democratic principles. These principles have been marred, and the integrity of our words questioned, because the world knows that even though we, the African diaspora, speak boldly we are not healed. Many leaders are convinced that Judeo-Christian values are relevant and necessary, but are unwilling to fully embrace them, because they wonder if the African diaspora will ever be healed.

People who are the descendants of African slaves have a tremendous opportunity to tell the world about God's desire for an atmosphere of unity, freedom and liberty in each nation, so that every man, woman and child may become what God created them to be. They will affirm that "the dream" was not "made in America or Europe." They have the potential to point out that leaders are responsible to provide the atmosphere that enables their people to pursue their righteous destiny. These principles will unleash untapped potentials.

The concept of all men being equal and endowed with inalienable rights is a God given principle taught by Jesus Christ in Nazareth and revealed by the Bible. Everyone deserves to be free. I also believe that everyone can handle freedom. No man gives another man true freedom. Superior powers do not really give other nations or peoples their freedom; they recognize it. We are born free. Freedom can be hindered, restricted, abused or ignored by others, but only the individual can give up his freedom.

Freedom is a birthright. It is a human right. It is for FREEDOM that Christ has made us free. The journey of people of African heritage is that all people – every ethnic group - qualify to be free.

Freedom is an approach to life. It is, at its greatest level, a spiritual experience. Then it becomes a mental attitude and finally a lived experience. The freedom to be what God has created the individual to be is a basic right of all. It is not an American trait. It is not given because it is in the United Nations' Human Rights charter. The Queen of England cannot give it. Governments merely acknowledge it. God is the one that gives freedom to all.

Freedom is a precious thing. It is costly. It is an internal commodity. According to the Webster's Dictionary, to be free means "having liberty, not being a slave, not controlled or influenced by others, independent." It is the ability to make up your own mind and then carry it out. It is a potent four-letter word: FREE.

Many governments today, sadly enough, many led by descendants of African slaves, are anti-freedom. They bind their own people. Many do not believe that the people they lead deserve freedom. Some leaders and national influencers conclude that the people in their nation are not sophisticated nor educated enough for freedom. They pontificate that the people are not ready for such western concept and so much responsibility. Some deliberately nurture group thinking and severely punish free thinkers and dissenters. Many use cultural heritage, history and nationalism as a scapegoat to have their own way: maintain power, money and personal legacy.

Freedom means to have the ability to act in such a way as to make your choice a reality. When you are free, you are willing to suffer the consequences of your choice. An ungodly society abuses freedom. The natural end is authoritarianism, which is what slavery was. Slavery was authoritarianism on steroids.

A slave is a person under the control of others. This control can be spiritual, emotional, economic, political and even mental. If a person is not able to implement their decision, is that person free?

Jesus declared, "You shall know the truth, and the truth will make you free" (John 8:32). You can be aware of the truth and still be bound. You can read it and still be bound. The truth does have the ability to make you free. However, it will take intimacy with the truth for a positive result. There must be a mind change, a change in perception and understanding that takes place when you accept the truth. Untruth must be unlearned, and then replaced by truth to have true personal freedom.

The writer of Romans said, "Do not be conformed to this world, but be transformed (get a make-over) by the renewing of your mind so that you can experience what is the good and perfect will of God" (Romans 12:2). Truth transforms. The Apostle Paul also wrote, "if any man be in Christ, he is a new creation; old things are passed away; and behold all things (are made) new" (2 Corinthians. 5: 17).

One of my childhood role models was Light Brigade Barrett. She was one of my childhood Sunday school teachers. She lived in England but returned to Jamaica to live and serve the Lord. She told me that once there was a member of the Church who told a lie on her. She was angry. She later prayed to forgive her, but every time she saw the lady, she felt a tug in her heart. This went on for a while until the Holy Spirit showed her that she was still tied to this lady. She needed to release herself. It took many days of prayer and fasting to get to the root of her un-forgiveness, but the inner freedom was worth it. She was free. She could see her offender without her blood pressure rising or even for that offense to be the main thing on her mind. She was able to work with her again.

When the truth about God, about Jesus, about the Holy Spirit, and about God's word is believed, it has the inherent power to break the mental strongholds and thought patterns. It heals the inner pain that hinders true freedom. The truth targets the lies we believe. The destruction of the lies we hold on to creates the space for the truth to be established in us. The destruction of the lies removes the toxic emotional attachment to the hurt. The destruction of lies eventually lead to healed emotions and wholesome memories of our life experiences. Decisions and actions taken based on the truth received will give the sweet success of victory, and new life is the result. The Bible calls it the "peaceable fruit of righteousness" (Hebrews 12:11).

Let me ask you; what are you afraid of? What are you avoiding? Are you afraid to be free? Freedom does not have any particular address or location. It flows from God to you and through you to others. Don't leave the altar until you have been made free.

The late reggae singer, Bob Marley sang, "emancipate yourself from mental slavery, none but ourselves can free our mind." He obviously realized that the root of the problem was internal; mental slavery. However, he was wrong about the solution. How can one free himself from this kind of slavery? If someone is suffering from mental slavery how could they have the capacity to come up with solutions that are wise and effective?

Unfortunately, many still blindly follow his leadership. Mental or inner freedom is not the "high" from smoking marijuana or other drugs. It is not a mental trip we take away from Babylon. It is not rebelling against society, dressing the way I want to, growing my hair wild, forming my own subculture or my own gang. It does not mean a carefree lifestyle. Doing whatever one feels like doing whenever, however and with whomever, are not signs of freedom. That is a description of bondage.

If you are tied to the latest trend and pop culture style, you are not free to live the way God created you to live. If you have to be hip, then you and your money are slaves to someone else. Someone figured out how to get you to work for them. They know how to get the money out of your pocket.

Mental slavery means that a certain philosophy or perspective dominates my thinking pattern and determines my worldview. It conditions people into a particular way of thinking and living. It relies heavily on emotions and uses false promises to capture the creativity of others. Freedom comes by identifying this pattern or stronghold and replacing it with the truth. "*You shall know the truth* [about you, your history, your pain, your present, your potential, and your future] *and the truth WILL MAKE YOU FREE*" (John 8:32)

Did you notice the promise is to be "made free?" It is a process. But, you start somewhere. God cannot make you, unless you allow Him to the opportunity to mold you. The scripture did not say that the truth would merely "set" you free; it clearly indicates that God is interested in more than your vote of confidence. God is not doing this simply for His own sake. He wants you to be free. He wants you to be free. He sets people free to make them free people. Not all free people are truly free. Unfortunately, there are many for whom the stench of the slave ships still lingers, and the crack of the "massa's" whip a present terror.

When they look in the mirror, many do not see a beautiful man or woman created in the image of the Almighty God, with potential and a unique destiny. How about you, what do you see? Do you find yourself preparing day after day for a fight? Do you feel like you need to represent your people? The way you see yourselves is the way you perceive that others see you. The way you believe others perceive you is the way you will see yourself. You will always respond to someone based on how you believe that you are perceived. The key is to shift focus. Look at something more important.

Parent, please do not try to motivate your child to succeed in school and life by using negative stereotypes of your race. Please do not tell your child that no one expects them to succeed or that they should work hard to "prove them wrong." That's a negative starting point. We may feel like blaming failure or lack of discipline on of the prejudices or discriminations we face in life, but that is not freedom, that's being bound to others opinion. We should work hard to succeed to honor our creator, not to compete or prove anything to anyone. Yes, we should be aware of what is aptly called the "soft bigotry of low expectation," and we should deal with it in law, in policy and as individuals. But you're under no obligation to earn approval from anyone. You are not obligated to prove anything to anyone. You are commanded to love, and to forgive. When you please God everything will be alright.

If we're not careful our entire life could be spent in the fight to deal with prejudice; the fight to prove oneself worthy of attention or the fight to be recognized. The inner struggle to smile and look happy while deep hurts and pain is building up on the inside, is at the root of many cases of depression, substance abuse, domestic violence and even suicide. The inner pain over our family history cries out for attention. There is bitterness, un-forgiveness, hopelessness, and anger, because there is no settlement in sight to the hurt about the killing and exploitation of loved ones. The feeling is real.

Have you ever listened to a washing machine that is stuck on the spin cycle? Round and round it goes. That's what many are facing right now: the mind and the soul is never at rest. Every waking hour is consumed by thoughts such as: I wonder what they're thinking; I have to show them I'm smart too; I have to represent my people; I have to do this, I have to do that...." Am I really accepted? Did they really mean that? Will I always be a minority? I can't believe this is my life. I better not trust them. Watch yourself! They don't mean it. Am I selling out on my people, if I try to break out of this cycle?"

Let's stop this. It's time to take back your mind. This is not a good way to live. It doesn't have to be that way. You can unclutter your head so that the creative and successful thoughts can come in. It's time to be healed.

## My Friend
### By Sam Burns

My friend, do you know Jesus, God's precious Sin?
Are you on your way to heaven, when your life is done?
Have you had your sins forgiven, are you basking in his love?
Are you walking in the Light that comes from above?

Do you thrill in His presence, as you read his precious word?
And does the voice of Jesus bring response to what you have
heard?
Do you linger in His presence as you pray from day to day?
Do your friends really listen to what you have to say?

Is your life a victory in a world of sin?
Are you making every effort your friends to win?
Are you trusting in His leading, as you do His perfect will?
When the lost turn to Jesus, does it give your heart a thrill?

When your life is over and you stand before the King,
Will He say, "Well Done." For the ones you helped to bring?

# Chapter 8

## Yes, You Can Be Healed.

Now is the time to be healed from all hurts and offenses, old and new. But how will you know when you are healed?

I believe that when you can remember the past, and experience peace and appreciation instead of feelings of ashamed, belittlement, angry or bitterness, then you have been healed. If your reflection produces admiration for the victories, the strength, courage and accomplishment of your fore parents, then you have entered your personal healing. You know that you are healed when you feel you have nothing to prove to anyone, except to love your Creator.

You know you are healed when you pay more attention to the awesome legacy of strength, wisdom, perseverance, creativity and Godliness of your heritage than the slights, hurts, insults, abuse and offenses you face in life. You know that you are healed when even names, so-called "dog whistles" and trigger statements no longer affect your emotions. The greatest victory is when the strategies that were used to destroy you become a blessing to you; for what the devil attempts with evil intentions, God uses for our good, over and over.

When you are healed you will also find great peace and joy in setting others free. It is amazing how God use people to help others to go through the very thing that they experienced. Your "mess" will give you a message. The apostle Peter was the greatest example of a turncoat. Yet after Jesus' resurrection, he was summoned. Christ told Peter that it was his responsibility to strengthen others after he had been strengthened. Likewise, we have an opportunity to strengthen others with the very help that we have received. Your potential lies within your pain.

You will be able to comfort others with the comfort with which you have been comforted in Christ Jesus. You will become a part of the greatest missionary force in the world. As you truly anchor your identity and future in God, settle your perception of your equality and worthiness, you will bring a depth of wisdom, care and insight to the places of decision making that will bring much glory to our God and help millions of people. Instead of making you bitter, your painful experiences will make you a better person. You will be full of great emotional intelligence. You will be able to connect with people in their pain. That attitude will enable the Church to be a stronger and more effective witness for Christ. It will open many doors for you.

We must choose to bury the hatchet and unleash our destiny. The Great Commission is at stake. Our Lord deserves finality. The next generation deserves this chance. It is the final leg of the journey. Jesus' solution is not too simplistic, is it? He believes that He has done enough to bring healing to every heart in every situation. Do you also believe? He makes it possible to forgive. Stop trying to forget; just choose to forgive.

You cannot expect the world, the governments, political systems, social parties, university systems, civil rights nor human rights movements to give healing and closure to the wounds of prejudice, slavery, racism, and discrimination. But we who are called Christians, because we have submitted to Christ Jesus as our Lord and King, can receive, initiate, teach, and exemplify healing. This new Godly perspective that I am encouraging is only made possible because of Jesus Christ.

The Christian message is an invitation to healing from all wounds through the bridge of forgiveness. The Rev. Dr. Martin Luther King Jr. called the concept of forgiveness "words lifted to cosmic proportion." Forgiving your enemies is possible. It is realistic. It is not idealistic. It is reasonable and right. Yes, forgiveness is possible. It is do-able. It is practical. Forgiveness is not just reserved for saints but flawed human beings like you and me.

We're not blind. Racism, prejudice, and discrimination will always exist on the earth, because sin will be on the earth until it is finally judged. It will never be legislated away. Law enforcement cannot erase it. Election cycles come and go. The curfews will end at some point. Like Yugoslavia, as soon as the dictator dies, people will resurrect hidden grudges and fight to win or at least to prove their point. We must accept that racism, prejudice, and discrimination are not "white" or exclusively European problem. It is a human problem. It equally exists among blacks, browns, yellows and all the mixture in between. It is a problem of the heart. It is called sin.

I have heard some say that people of African descent cannot be racist, because they do not have the power to enforce anything. That is not so true anymore, is it? We do have power.

We should not change the normal meaning of words to fit our point. What is racism? What is prejudice? What is discrimination? These are neutral words. They describe attitudes not people. No one has a corner on these descriptive words. For these words to be taken seriously their definitions must remain universal. Can you imagine the chaos of trying to redefine "upward" as "downward?" We're seeing the result of that approach around the world. You don't need power, money, wealth or opportunity to develop a wrong heart. Sin knows no color.

Let's consider the word "racism." The Webster's Dictionary defines race as "a group of people of common ancestry or division recognized as a distinct human type and characterized by inherited traits." Racism is defined as "a belief that certain races of men are, by birth and nature or features, superior to others." It is being a respecter of one race or partial to one race to the disadvantage or exclusion of others. It is placing a greater value or importance on one person over another based on race.

115

I'm not encouraging you to ignore your race nor your roots. We all need these connections. We should all place a high value on our historical, cultural and racial heritage. However, we should aim to grow beyond our roots. Branches bear fruits, not roots, however the roots are necessary to support the branches, it doesn't control the branches. I would argue that like a tree, it is the fruits, and not the roots, that defines it. And so while we honor and acknowledge someone's roots we should never use that fact alone to make assumptions about them. Similar trees also have different quality of fruits.

Discrimination means, "To make a distinction in favor of or against one person or thing as compared to others." To see and note the racial difference of a person, and then to use that as the basis of making a decision against them is called racial discrimination.

The word prejudice refers to "injury or damage due to judgment or action of another; a favoring or dislike of something (or someone) without just grounds or before sufficient knowledge; an irrational attitude of hostility directed against an individual, a group or a race." It means to pre-judge (and sentence) someone before holding a proper trial or inquiry. It is not giving the individual a fair chance to present him or herself as they see fit. To be prejudice means having a certain mindset, a closed mind or a "made up mind" about an individual, and in this context, simply because of the color of his or her skin.

Nothing is wrong with judging on the basis of righteous principles. In fact, that is expected of us. But color, race or a person's ethnic history does not really tell who that person is. We should respect each other's individuality. Consequently, anyone can be racist, prejudicial or discriminatory. It is a condition of the heart, not skin. Anyone can be affected by it.

Emotional and spiritual baggages due to our history and experiences, must be dealt with deliberately. Healing and forgiveness does not mean to ignore the wrongs, stifle the pain, nor belittle the hurts. The key to healing is first of all to acknowledge the root of the problem, then to turn to God and receive His grace to be healed from it. The doctor will have a hard time helping you if you refuse to be honest about the real problem.

David experienced healing after suffering great pain. In Psalm 103: 1-2 he declared, "Bless the Lord, O my soul and all that is within me bless His Holy name. Bless the Lord O my soul and forget not all His benefits."

God is in the business of healing and restoring our souls. We must release the past to embrace the future. He promises healing of our soul now, not just in the sweet by and by. In the next chapter I will show you how to access this healing for your soul.

To "bless the Lord" means to praise, make God happy, to adore, to speak well of, or to heap "kudos" upon the Lord the way you would on someone you love and admire. Nothing "blesses" a father more than to see his children handle problems the way in which he taught them. Nothing "blesses" God more than to see you react with the right attitude.

The greatest need we have is to learn to bless with our souls. The soul is unseen. It is our personhood and individuality. It consist of the mind – our thinking faculties; the emotions – the feeling faculties; and the will – the decision making part of our being. The soul is tender and impressionable. The body interacts with the world around us using the five senses to inform the soul about our environment. This is done at a speed faster than the speed of light.

There is another part of mankind, which is vital to the health of the soul and body; the spirit. Your spirit is the area of communication, intuition and worship. Your spirit receives from God and communicates with the soul for a final decision. For the Christian, the spirit is alive and functions as the center of his being. For the unsaved, the soul assumes that role until the spirit is reconciled or rejoined to God. This opportunity for reconnection or new life through accepting Jesus' substitution for us, is the good news of salvation.

Your soul plays a vital role in how you deal with the experiences of life. The state of your soul maps out the state of your life. It is the center of all memories, and emotions. It is where hurts are stored. It is where the reaction to fight, to curse or forgive starts. Memories- good and bad - become a part of our soul. When the Bible encourages us to "bless" the Lord with our soul, it is an invitation to consciously give our spirit more influence over what goes on in our soul.

The human spirit needs more influence over your soul than your five senses. You are becoming more like what God created you to be when you pay more attention to the communication coming out of your spirit than what you feel or sense with your five senses Following your emotions and feelings more than the wisdom coming from your spirit makes you a more "soulish" or as the Bible calls it a "fleshly" person. That simply means that your life is mostly influenced by the things you see, feel, remember, etc., more than by Godly principles. This is important. The difference between "soulish" versus "spirit" led living is like building your house on the sand versus the rock. A soulish or sandy foundation leads to anxiety. It causes us to be easily manipulated by those who know how to trick your five senses, exploit of emotions, bend our will and use deception to have their way.

The soul has to be constantly cleansed, examined, and renewed with the word of truth (this is the purpose for the Bible). If not, we become overloaded. This happens when the soul is constantly bombarded with information from all five senses, including our memory, emotions, and thoughts all requiring a response. Have you ever been emotionally over loaded? Depressions, stress, anger and many illnesses follows.

David knew what it meant for his soul to be troubled. In Psalm 42:2-3 he said, "My soul thirsts for God, for the living God.

When shall I come and appear before God? My tears have been my food day and night, while they continually say to me, "Where is your God?"

Later as a fugitive hiding in the cave and running from his own king, the great King Saul, he wrote, "No one cares for my soul..." (Psalm 142). Have you been to a place where your friends and everything familiar is gone, and your soul enters into a twilight zone? And you feel like no one cares for your soul? I have.

When I left Jamaica in 1999, I had no idea what to do about my future. My soul cried out bitterly, because everything that was familiar to me was gone. Many friends and associates that I thought were close were gone. I felt deeply betrayed. In that season of your life, you cannot depend on what you see, feel, hear or remember to guide you into the future. My family and I prayed, and we consciously decided to pay more attention to what God was saying to our spirit man. What was God saying in the Bible that applied to the current situation?

Little by little I found the path into my future. It began with forgiveness. I had to choose to let my soul bless the Lord. I had to start when things were bad. It was only then that my circumstances began to change. I changed my future when I forgave those who trespassed against me.

Jesus is able to identify with the issues that haunt your soul and crowd your thoughts. He was "A man of sorrows and acquainted with grief" (Isaiah 53: 3). God truly understands you.

You might recognize your own grief in this description of Christ by Isaiah:

All we like sheep have gone astray; We have turned, every one, to his own way; And the Lord has laid on Him the iniquity of us all....Yet it pleased the Lord to bruise Him; He has put Him to grief. When You make His soul an offering for Sin..

119

…He poured out His soul unto death, And He was numbered with the transgressors, And He bore the sin of many, And made intercession for the transgressors (Isaiah 53:12).

You have been like a childless woman, but now you can sing and shout for joy. Now you will have more children than a woman whose husband never left her.

Make the tent you live in larger; lengthen its ropes and strengthen the pegs! You will extend your boundaries on all sides; your people will get back the land that the other nations now occupy. Cities now deserted will be filled with people.

Do not be afraid-you will not be disgraced again; you will not be humiliated. You will forget your unfaithfulness as a young wife, and your desperate loneliness as a widow. Your Creator will be like a husband to you- the Lord Almighty is His name. The holy God of Israel will save you- He is the ruler of all the world…..

You are like a young wife, deserted by her husband and deeply distressed. But the Lord calls you back to Him and says: "For one brief moment I left you; with deep love I will take you back. I turned away angry for only a moment, but I will show you My love forever." So says the Lord who saves you. "In the time of Noah I promised never again to flood the earth. Now I promise not to be angry with you again; I will not reprimand or punish you. The mountains and hills may crumble, but My love for you will never end; I will keep forever My promise of peace." So says the Lord who loves you.

The Lord says, "O …you suffering, helpless city, with no one to comfort you, I will rebuild your foundations with precious stones. I will build your towers with rubies, your gates with stones that glow like fire, and the wall around you with jewels. I myself will teach your people and give them prosperity and peace. Justice and right will make you strong.

You will be safe from oppression and terror. Whoever attacks you, does it without My consent; whoever fights against you will fall. "I create the blacksmith, who builds a fire and forges weapons. I also create the soldier, who uses the weapons to kill. But no weapon will be able to hurt you; you will have an answer for all who accuse you. I will defend My servants and give them victory." The Lord has spoken" (Isaiah 54:1-17 - Today's English Version).

Job also had some troubles in his life. He lost his children. He lost his property and place. He lost his friends. He was falsely accused. It was important for his well-being that he remained in relationship with God.

He poured out his soul in the middle of his affliction and said:

I am tired of living. Listen to my bitter complaint. Don't condemn me, God. Tell me! What is the charge against me? Is it right for you to be so cruel? To despise what you yourself have made? And then to smile on the schemes of wicked people? Do you see things as we do? Is your life as short as ours? Then why do you track down all my sins and hunt down every fault I have? You know that I am not guilty, that no one can save me from you. (Job 10:1-7, Today's Living Version).

Job struggled with God and even questioned God's ability to understand what he was going through. Job's experience is not unfamiliar. I can identify with his reaction.

As a boy, my mother and I lived with her uncle in St. Thomas. To me, Mr. Lester Reid (Uncle Lester), the Royal Air Force Veteran, was my hero. He was a hard worker, business man and a great man in the way he treated people and in his personal character. He was a deacon at our Church. He built a nice home and added another building to the property and opened up his own store in Yallahs, St. Thomas. He ran his own business as long as I can remember. In fact that was how my mother ended up in St. Thomas. They closed one business in Kingston to start another in St. Thomas. He was the bright light to the members of both the Reid and Waite family.

In 1980 cruel men ended his life prematurely on what started out as an ordinary Saturday evening. I was just a teenager then. One group of thieves came into our house and held us hostage, while another team took over the store. Our store was like a small haberdashery shop where you could find everything from bicycle parts to staple food supplies. My mother was in the shop when the robbers came. She survived by running out and praying the Lord's Prayer out loud as she ran. However, many in our family still believe that this was a planned hit on Uncle Lester. He was the only one who was shot. The killers took a few items from the store and left the money untouched.

I was gun-butted and ordered to the ground. I was later pushed into one of the bedrooms with the barrel of a gun in my face. However, that ordeal was nothing compare to the shock and pain that entered my world when I ran outside and saw Uncle Lester lying face down in the dirt. He was dead. My soul was overwhelmed with sorrow, anger and rage all at once. The killers where never caught. For years the anger and bitterness ate away at my soul. In fact the pain is still fresh for many in our family today. However, as I learned the ways of Jehovah God I realized that He wanted me to forgive the killers even though I had no idea who they were.

This was hard because a plan was already taking shape in my mind to locate some weapons and exact my own justice, even if that meant joining the army.

I eventually learnt that forgiveness was the only way to be healed. I realized that my future would be determined by my response to this great offense. I could either have a twisted future or a free flowing future. Forgiveness was God's way. So I did. I forgave them without ever meeting them, and without even waiting for them to ask for forgiveness. Today the memory of the incident does not fill me with pain, anger or un-forgiveness. I still have the loss, but I celebrate the life of Uncle Lester and hope to live up to his standards today.

Year later as I traveled through the Norman Manley Airport in Kingston, I met a lady from our little community in St. Thomas. She knew my uncle and the entire story about his murder, and that no one was ever charged. She pulled me aside to inform me that the alleged murderer and ringleader was killed in a gunfight with the police.

I was surprised by my reaction. I did not cheer. It was almost as if justice had already been done in my eyes from the time I forgave the killer. And so hearing this news was like old news. It really didn't change anything for me. I was free from this individual a long time ago. He did not pull my trigger. I was already free from the hurt of the incident years before. I believe this is an often-overlooked benefit of being a Christian. We have access to "*peace that passes all understanding*" (Philippians 4:17).

Forgiveness is a decision not an emotion. We honor God by forgiving others of their offenses against us. Forgiveness is a legal action. It means to surrender our right to personally exact judgment and punishment. It's turning over the case to the rightful authority.

Forgiving someone is like bringing a case against an offender in the court of law. You have a bulging folder with all the evidences. You have witnesses. You have the fingerprints. You have compelling and irrefutable evidences that the offender is guilty. You have a good case. However, you are not the judge. Your responsibility is to present the case, and then turn over the folder and leave it to the judge to make the final judgment and set the sentencing. If you believe that the judge is tainted and compromised then you may have a reason to not let it go, but if you trust the judge, you should allow him to deal with the case. They have jurisdiction over it. In fact, the more you meddle with your case the more you will delay your day of justice.

When you forgive those involved in injustices and the hurts inflicted on your fore parents, you are letting go of the case. But you are not letting it go into thin air. You are turning it over to the Judge, who is also your Heavenly Father. He cares for you and loves you like the 'apple of His very eyes.' Justice will be served when you forgive.

In the Psalms David choose to anchor his soul in the Lord. He said, "I will bless the Lord at all times: His praise shall continually be in my mouth. My soul shall make her boast in the Lord: the humble shall hear thereof, and be glad. O magnify the Lord with me, and let us exalt His name together" (Psalm 34:1-3).

Your song is connected with the condition of your soul. The song will change when the soul is healed. When you forgive, your soul now "*makes her boast* (expresses confidence or faith*) in the Lord.*" It starts with a choice, "*I will.*" This decision must be based on obedience to the truth. It requires faith, which is trusting in God's direction above what you feel. And you do have faith. We make decisions all the time based on the words of people we trust. God certainly has something to tell you which is worth trusting. His track record is worthy of your confidence.

A lot of the music and songs that we hear today are "soulish." The styles may vary, but they address issues in the mind, will or emotions (the soul) or experienced by the human senses (the body). They may tell the story of real experiences or desires in life, but they are not necessarily telling the whole truth. If it is void of the spiritual or divine perspective, then it cannot be wholesome. Soul music is the yearning or the longing of the soul. It is about feelings, emotions, your thoughts and the decisions we make. Musicians today are peddling the same soul story, just a different style of music. Soul music is a mere commentary on the world around us. But what about the songs of the spirit?

Soul music is not what David was referring to when He said, "Bless the Lord Oh my soul." A different song was coming from David's soul, because he dared to believe God's perspective on the issues of his life. His Godly perspective influenced the lyrics of his song. His soul was now mostly influenced by his spirit, which was now influenced by the Holy Spirit, because David had a restored relationship with His Creator. The music style is not the issue, the heart and content is. King David was a Psalmist or a singer. He found a lot to praise God for, and so should we, regardless of what we are going through and what others are saying or doing.

Psalm 103:1-5 gives a glimpse of some of the benefits that comes to our lives when we praise God, or as David said, "bless" the Lord.

The first benefit is your own *forgiveness*. Have you ever felt the freedom of forgiveness? The moment when your conscience is washed clean of guilt is amazing. It is one thing to "get away with something." It feels like a brand new day when you know that you are guilty, only to have the issue settled, and the mercy of forgiveness.

Another benefit is the healing and restoration of our bodies. The Lord also *"redeems your life from destruction."* Soulish living sets us on a pathway of destruction. The psycho-physiological connection of many illnesses is an area of study that many are paying attention to now. Many scientists are recognizing that the condition of our soul affects our physical health. There are not only spiritual, but mental and physical consequences when truth is ignored. The word "redemption" speaks of "buying something back." Through faith in Jesus we all get another chance at life after being sold down a destructive path.

I met a young man in Port Charlotte, Florida from the nation of Guyana. He was taking a smoke break from his shift at a McDonald's restaurant. I struck up a conversation with him and asked him about his plans for the future. He basically told me that he was just trying to live and make a life. He had no time for Church. His mother was dead. His father was in another state. He used to attend Church when he was young, but didn't really see the benefit of it now. He agreed with me that it was a "jungle out there." Those whom he thought were his friend are now too busy for him. He was just trying to be his own man. His response was a reminder that we need to take the time to point out the benefits of living life by faith in Christ. Many people miss the benefits of faith in Christ.

He needed guidance. The Bible gives the guidance which he needed. The Bible is full of wisdom for all young men. It states that even when our mothers and fathers forsake us, the Lord will adopt us as His own, and guide us through life. Can you imagine what our cities would be like if our young men could connect with the benefits of forgiveness?

Another benefit of living God's way is that He *"crowns you with loving kindness and tender mercies."* There is a measure of tenderness and kindness that enter our lives when we are more spiritually focused. There is more love, because love begets love. When we do things God's way we will have an unconditional, never ending supply of love, because God is love. Being merciful is a sign of humility. We are merciful to others because we understand the frailty and sinful heart of man. We are merciful to others even when they offend us, because we agree that "there goes I but for the grace of God." Kindness and being merciful attracts even more of the same. Proverbs 18:24 states that "a man that hath friends must shew himself friendly: and there is a friend that sticketh closer than a brother."

The benefits continue: He "*satisfies your mouth with good things so that your youth is renewed like an eagle.*" Living a spirit-led life is truly enriching and rejuvenating. It will enable you to rise above the storm like an eagle. This way of living renews your youthfulness. It builds resiliency. Old age and sickness is not brought on due to stress. Forgiving others is good for your health.

David finished the list of benefits by stating, "*The Lord executes righteousness and justice for all who are oppressed.*" This information should remove all fear of the future. It should eliminate every hesitation to forgive those who caused you harm. The Lord, our King, promised to make sure that the right thing is done by you. He is promising you justice. Trust in God. He guarantees that you will win and live to enjoy the victory as long as you live to do His will. The will of God for your life is simply that you obey the word of God. It means to be where God can find you.

One of the greatest truth that I have learned in my life is that God is just. Sometimes it seems like those with money, influence, connections or from the "right" neighbors or the "right ethnic group" have the advantage, however those who follow God's direction will be vindicated. When you forgive you are allowing God to bring true justice into the situation. That's when you understand the real game and appreciate who the real winners are. You will win with God by your side.

Many people live from Monday to Friday following the guidance of their souls (soulish living), but then seek peace at a church service on the weekends. They listen to the Spirit of God for that one-day, unfortunately, once Sunday service is over, the soul takes control again. This is not God's plan; neither is this a good plan. This is not a winning approach to life. It is possible to be born again, saved and filled with the Holy Ghost, and yet not experience life as God planned it, because of problems within the soul. God is ready, but we also need to be ready. Cooperation is required, because we have the freedom of choice.

God wants us to live on earth following the guidance of the Holy Spirit who communes with our spirit. We must live by the Spirit and not our soul (natural perception). To miss this principle is to hold yourself back and delay numerous blessings in your life. Don't risk it.

Songs are good, but they do not heal. Songs help to change the mood, and lift our attention beyond the pain. We need new songs that point to healing and assist in the healing. There are some songs which we should definitely stop singing. Why sing songs that have no relevance to the present leg of the journey? I can understanding singing those songs at times of remembrance and honoring of the past. Sorrowful songs dampen the soul and sap the energy to live. We need relevant songs. The songs of the cotton field and plantations were good for that time. It is time to write and sing songs that exalt the answers to the problems of today — songs that point to the higher purposes and generational goals of this time. The songs should promote harmony. Let's change the songs to match the vision for the future.

Forgiveness is the first step towards finding new songs and new styles of music. It is the beginning of healing and wholeness. When you forgive you allow the supernatural power of God to go deep in your own heart to remove the sting of the offense and heal the inner wound. You will know that you are healed when you will remember the incidents and even discuss it without stirring up the same raw emotion that existed before. Feelings of anger, hurt, resentment, and vengeance will be replaced by peace and a sense of "settledness" and moving on.

To be healed means that the incident, because it has lost its place of dominance over you, will soon fade away into the past, where it truly belongs. When healing comes then the offense will no longer be the most important issue between you and that person. That issue will not define the terms of the present and future interaction and the relationship. It will not be the big elephant in the room sucking up all the oxygen and presiding over every conversation. You will eventually have to force yourself to even remember the offense.

You'll know that you're healed when race is not the number one issue or default topic of our conversations, songs and works of arts. You'll know that you are healed when you no longer use race as an automatic filter of your response to an event or incident.

There are so many new things that will happen in your life after old wounds are healed and unresolved issues are settled within your own heart. We would start addressing topics that are more current at our family gatherings and social meetings. Family gatherings might even become a time to discuss new ideas and ways to help another family member to start a business, go to college, etc. A major benefit will be that the issue of race will no longer be the silent influencer of your decisions and lifestyle. Healing means peace with God, peace within our own hearts, and hopefully peace with man. It is possible to forgive, have peace with God, even if the offender remains offensive. They no longer pull your trigger. That's because you don't need their permission or cooperation to forgive them. Forgiveness is your choice. Forgiveness is about you taking back control of your future. It is about how you chose to deal with their offensive behavior. It's not up to them. They're not in control. God is in control.

Healing also means that you will be able to interact with people of the same color, ethnicity or culture as those who offended you without placing any expectation or burden of past wrongs on them. If you forgive those who caused harm to you and your fore parents, then the issue is settled. When you forgive you're removing the emotional baggage that could overshadow present relationships. It literally takes the bitter aftertaste out of your mouth. It brings relief from the mental pressure of second-guessing and worrying about your approval by others. It takes away the unnatural sensitivity to the opinion or attitude of others. It frees you from being the thought and motive police. You no longer need to "represent."

The mental limits of what you may aspire to do will forever be removed. The permission lid will be lifted. When you have experienced this healing you will be liberated to think free and live free. You will be free to make the decisions which you truly desire to make about your future. You will have the mindset to embrace your destiny. You live where you need to live to do what you need to do. Your concern will go beyond asking questions like: How many of "our people are here? Will I be allowed? Am I accepted? Do they really mean it? What are they doing behind closed doors to stop me?"

One of the greatest benefits of this way of life is that once we have deliberately dealt with the issues of our past hurts and injustices, then we'll be able to communicate that same attitude of forgiveness to our children and the future generations. The result will be a new attitude for life, a new spirit of freedom, new opportunities, entrepreneurship and a new ownership attitude in our communities. Only then will Rev. Dr. Martin Luther King Jr's dream become a reality for you.

Globalization makes it possible for people to interact with others from diverse ethnic and cultural backgrounds. However, just the mere opportunity to meet others does not make people less inhibited by others. Unless these issues facing the African diaspora are settled then globalization will only make the problem worse. Globalization in an unsettled environment will lead to more extreme steps towards isolation for preservation. In fact, if you are very sensitive to cultural, ethnic or historical wrongs, you will have a problem building quality relationships in this era. Unresolved issues will make it difficult for you to step outside your community. You will find your world shrinking.

In globalization the rich and informed are able move freely around the world absorbing assets and opportunities everywhere while those whose fore parents built the infrastructure for prosperity are unable and often unprepared to participate, not because of barriers, but because they have not forgiven their offenders. Globalization also means the introduction of new players from different cultures with their own biases and prejudices. So the offensives will increase, making forgiveness even more important. There will always be some form of barriers in life, but the African diaspora have already overcome the worst part of it. We overcome the rest through forgiveness.

In Florida I saw kids play together from kindergarten all the way up to high school. Then as they begin high school the pressure to choose racial camps increase. You can often see the formation in the school cafeterias. Extreme pressure is placed on anyone who try to walk their own path, unless it is some extreme lifestyle choice. In fact those who choose "alternate" life styles are given more respect than those who refuse to fall in line with the racial camps. The same scenario is true across the Caribbean and the western hemisphere. These high schoolers become citizens and form the culture of our nations.

They become parents and teach that culture to their children (black and white). Remember that culture is more often caught, and not taught. Those assumed beliefs, unspoken cues and impression that we communicate about the way things are and what life has to offer, are more impressionable on our children that the words we speak.

The relationships between the different racial camps usually deteriorates to racial slurs and put downs of others, stereotypes or the silent treatment of avoidance. Why? Because hurt people, hurt people. Simply spending time around someone doesn't mean that you have buried the hatchet. It doesn't mean that you have resolved unsettled issues with their "kind." It does not mean that you want to relate or know how to relate to them. Forgiveness must be direct. There must be a deliberate and conscious effort to be healed from the feelings of hurts, discrimination and rejection.

There must be a paradigm shift in your thinking. I'm encouraging a radical change in approach to your interaction with people and to life. Once you are healed, the challenge becomes focused on doing God's will. His opinion rules over all others and becomes your source and rock. It gives your life focus. It gives you just one person to "worry about."

It is impossible to hear God and make wise decision when hurtful and unsettled issues dominate your thoughts and emotions. It is not your fault that you are hurt or that these issues exist. You may not be able to stop a bird from landing on your head, but you can stop it from building a nest. You cannot afford to give the power over your future into the hands of others. Prosperity, creativity, good health, and blessings will flow for many generations when your soul is healed. It's time for healing.

*Beloved, I wish above all things that you may prosper and be in health, even as your soul prospers* (3 John 1:2).

*The discretion of a man makes him slow to anger, and his glory is to overlook a transgression* (Proverbs 19:11).

## It's all in the state of Mind
Author Unknown

If you think you are beaten, you are
If you think that you care not, you don't,
If you'd like to win, but you think you can't,
It's almost certain you won't.
If you think you'll lose, you've lost,
For out in the world you'll find
Success begins with a fellows will – It's all in the state of mind.

Full many a race is lost
Ere even a step is run,
And many a coward falls
Ere even his work's begun.
Think big, and your deeds will grow;
Think small, and you'll fall behind;
Think that you can and you will -It's all in the state of mind.

If you think you are outclassed, you are;
You've got to think high to rise;
You've got to be sure of yourself before
You can ever win a prize.
Life's battles don't always go
To the stronger or faster man;
But soon or late the man who wins
Is the man who thinks he can.

# Chapter 9

## How to Do Forgiveness

Do you believe that it is impossible for you to forgive those who enslaved your fore parents, and those who offended you? God believes that you can. I agree with God. This is a good place us to say, "Yes, we can!"

The Bible communicates God's heart on this matter. We can forgive from the heart. To truly forgive is a great virtue. Someone rightly said that it was better to forgive too much than to condemn too much.

Matthew chapter 18 shows us how to do forgiveness. Jesus did not dodge Peter's question about how to forgive someone who caused him great personal hurt. From the context of the story, it appears that this individual repeatedly and maliciously offending him. That person was getting on his last nerve. He had extended the olive branch of forgiveness to them before, only to have the offense repeated. Peter wanted to know whether this Godly perspective worked. He was running out of patience and wanted to know how many offenses was a reasonable amount to put up with. He must have tolerated this problem beyond the normal limits.

The Bible tells us later that when Christ was assaulted by the Romans soldiers in Gethsemane, Peter had a sword and he used it. He chopped off ear of one of the Romans soldiers.. By the way, I'm sure that he was not aiming for more than the Roman soldier's ear. Peter was serious when he inquired about the Christian way of handling repeated offenders. He could cut somebody.

Peter want to know if there was a point at which it was unrealistic to forgive. As usual our Lord's response took us beyond revenge or feeling bad, to the point of healing and true relationship. He helped Peter to deal with the real issue. The real issue was that Peter wanted justice, and he was not sure that forgiveness equaled justice. The descendants of African slaves who have suffered loss, discrimination, racial attacks, prejudice, and other forms of injustice want justice. And that is a good thing. If we know that justice is being served then we can be at peace.

Jesus instructed Peter to forgive without measure. He told Peter to forgive *"seventy times seven"* that is a total of 490 times! However, the lesson here is not to encourage score keeping. The lesson is to have a forgiving heart. The word on the street is to "do worse to others than what they have done to you, so that they will know not think to do it again" or "never forgive a transgression more than three times!"

Well, that is why Jesus is different. He is called the Prince of Peace, and those who follow Him are blessed to enjoy inner peace and to be peacemakers. You have a choice to make. Whose advice will you follow?

It is not honest to say that this principle does not work, unless you have genuinely tried it. I know many people who can testify that it works. And you can see the fruits in their lives and that of their descendants. They are happy. They are healed. They are free. If we demand an eye for an eye, we'll all end up blind!

Jesus followed up on his instructions to Peter with the parable of the Unforgiving Servant. In the parable, a servant who had a long history of wrongdoings was totally forgiven by his master. However, the same servant refused to forgive one of his fellow servants for their wrongs. In fact, he did the opposite. He took his fellow servant, who was indebted to him, to the courts and demanded full payment. It seemed like the concept of forgiving his fellow servant did not even cross his mind. The master was very angry because of this attitude. So he arrested the servant. Charged him for all the wrong things which he did, and delivered him to the tormentors.

Jesus then said this to Peter, "So My heavenly Father also will do to you if each of you FROM HIS HEART does not forgive his brother his trespasses*" (Matthew 18:15, capitalization mine).

I have been people asked many times, "how do you know they mean it when they ask you to forgive them? Or even "nobody ever told me they were sorry!" Jesus also addressed this by saying, "whatever you bind on earth will be bound in heaven, and whatever you loose on earth will be loosed in heaven. Again I say to you that if two of you agree on earth concerning anything that they ask, it will be done for them by My Father in heaven. For where two or three are gathered together in my name, I am there in the midst of them" (Matthew 18:18-20).

There are two important things to bear in mind from these scriptures. The first is that the condition of your heart is between you and God. The intention of someone else's heart is also between them and God. If they repent, you have a decision to make. If they do not repent, you still have a decision to make. You have a choice to either forgive or not from your heart. The condition of someone else's heart is also between them and God. Yes, their heart must be right, but that's their business, not yours. Your concern is the response of your own heart. We have enough problems discerning the condition and motive of our own heart.

You have the ability to deal with offenses even without the offender apologizing to you. If you only react to the action of your offender, then you're actually giving the offender the control of your emotions and your future. You will remain tied to your offender until you cut the cord, on your terms: forgiveness. You can change your future by forgiving.

Many believers quote Matthew 18:18-20 in the context of spiritual warfare - binding and loosing the devil. However, the context does not support this conclusion. The "binding and loosing" has to do with our response when our brother sins against us.

I submit that the "binding" refers to the emotional entanglement between you and your offender due to un-forgiveness, while the "loosing" is the forgiving or letting go of the offense and the offender. It's like tying a goat to a pole. The rope (of un-forgiveness or unhealed hurt) limits its freedom. You will always be tied to the person you refuse to forgive. Holding on to hurts and offenses continue the bondage. It is literally like walking around with a dead man on your back. His stench will affect everything that you come in contact with.

Jesus' response to Peter's question, and his lesson on the parable of the unforgiving servant, shows that those who were offended should take the first step. Don't wait on others; deal with the offense in a Godly way. God has no legal basis to stop the advance of the tormentor and bring true justice to the situation, if we harbor un-forgiveness.

It is possible to deal firmly and decisively with issues of racial discriminations, prejudice and racism without harboring un-forgiveness towards the offenders. It's not an either or proposition. Regardless of your view on reparations and the treatment of the slaves after the abolition of slavery, we must in all honesty admit that there have been some significant steps taken to address inequalities since the 1960s. There is certainly more to be done. However, there have been numerous reconciliation movements and conference, as well as volumes of new laws, legislation and court cases. Actual apologies have been given in Parliaments, Congress, and from pulpits all over the Western Hemisphere. Millions of people died in the USA civil war over the issue of slavery. So why do we need more apologies and positive overtures?

The Lord showed us the principle in the Lord's Prayer in Matthew chapter 6 *"...Give us this day our daily bread and forgive us our debts (trespasses or sins) as we forgive our debtors (*those who trespass against us).*"* Notice the phrase: as we forgive. Forgiveness holds the power of determination in this prayer. The promise of forgiveness is conditional. The Lord ties forgiveness for our personal sins to our willingness to forgive those who offend us. Our daily bread depends on it. The will of God being done on earth as it is in heaven depends on it. Freedom from temptation and the evil one is tied to our choice to forgive. Victorious living depends on forgiving those who hurt us and hurt those we love.

Forgiveness is for your freedom. Forgiveness is also for your protection. Forgiveness is for your health. It is about securing the future. Your destiny is affected. The Apostle Paul counseled the Corinthian Church as they faced a similar problem. He told them:

> For to this end I also wrote, that I might put you to the test, whether you are obedient in all things. Now whom you forgive anything, I also forgive. For if indeed I have forgiven anything, I have forgiven that one for your sakes in the presence of Christ, **lest Satan should take advantage of us**; for we are not ignorant of his devices"
> (2 Corinthians 2:9-11).

The enemy of mankind will gain an advantage wherever un-forgiveness is entertained. In the parable, the servant who refused to forgive was thrown to the tormenters. And that is exactly what happens when we refuse to forgive. We become tormented. There is mental and emotional torment, and unsettledness. The irony is that we will eventually take on the very characteristics of those we refuse to forgive. We become like whatever we focus on. If you focus on the offence of others, you will become like them!

Forgiveness also sets up a better future for our children. It hinders the devil from having grounds to influence their thinking, their aspirations and ultimately their lives. The Holy Spirit will enable you to do the impossible.

You can be saved from a dark and tormenting life of un-forgiveness. To refuse to forgive is to choose to live with the consequences of someone else's sin. You will have to live, however you have a choice as to whether or not you will live in torment and bitterness of soul, or in the freedom of forgiveness. This is not "letting them off the hook" it is literally letting yourself off the hook. It is neither rationalizing the issue nor covering it up.

You forgive for your own sake, not for someone else's. Forgiveness is between you and God, and no one else. When you forgive you activate God's justice system on your behalf.

Forgiveness is a decision not an emotion. You honor God by forgiving others of their offenses against you. It is a legal action. It means to surrender your right to enact judgment and punishment. It is turning over the case to the rightful authority. He has jurisdiction.

Trust in the Lord, and don't let the defeated devil get an advantage of you. The thief will stir up problems to distract you spiritually. He is trying to set you up. He is coming to kill your potential, rob you of your dreams and destroy your promise. Don't let him. Forgive. It's time to be healed.

Un-forgiveness is man's way of being in control. It is trying to be prosecutor, judge and jury and execution. It is really trying to be a god. I encourage you to stop trying to play god. It is not your responsibility to judge and punish all wrong doers. You would never have any time to dream, pray, plan, study, enjoy your relationships, and just plain live.

The following steps will change your life forever. It is a simple invitation for you to forgive. What happens in your heart and life is between you and your Creator. I'm simply encouraging you to choose to open up your heart, and be honest with Him. In return He will create something new in you. He will activate His justice system for you and your descendants. Your decision to forgive those who have impacted your life negatively will also have a positive impact on your descendants. So it is very important that you own this. You must be willing to do this to take the following steps.

**Step 1: Find a mentor or a supporter of your journey to forgiveness.**

I suggest that you ask a Pastor or a mature Christian to walk with you through these steps, but that is not a requirement. Embracing forgiveness means that you will have to confront some issues that you might have stored away deep in your soul and memories. You would benefit from having the support of others who understand your desire and commitment to be a "forgiver" or of someone who has taken this step before.

## Step 2: Set aside at least 30 minutes of private time.

Don't rush. You will need to be in a place where you are not distracted. You will need a Bible, a pen and a notebook.

Follow these steps to freedom. You're not alone. Remember, God is with you. The Holy Spirit is your Helper. We're praying for you.

## Step 3: Read the parable of the unforgiving servant in Matthew 18:21-35

## Step 4: Begin your time of prayer by verbalizing to God that you are willing to deal with the offenses heaped upon you and your ancestors His way.

In prayer, affirm that you understand that the root of all these wicked acts is sin. Sin motivated brothers and sisters to exploit their siblings. Acknowledge that you recognize that your real enemy is Satan, not people. Acknowledge that you are now willing to look to Him to get justice.

Verbalize before God that you understand that un-forgiveness is also a trick of the defeated devil to keep you in bondage and torment. You should also acknowledge before God that un-forgiveness is a sin of disobedience to His will, but that you are now ready to obey His word.

**Step 5: It's now time to be specific. Make a list as the Holy Spirit brings the names, issues, and incidents to your memory.**

Ask God to bring to your mind the people and issues that have offended you directly or indirectly. If it's important for you to be free from it, then be specific about it.
Identify the offenses. What is the wound? Your forgiveness will deal with the emotional pain caused by the offense of slavery, discrimination, prejudice, slur, etc. Described it. Give it a name and write it down. Take your time.

Verbalize to the Lord how you believe that those offenses affected you? You don't have to cover it up anymore. It is now time for healing. Confront the issue. Speak out loud so you can hear yourself say it.

Write down the words that have pierced your soul. They will be exposed, mentioned and dislodged by forgiveness.

This is a difficult, but necessary step. Your enemy lives in darkness. He often deceives us to believe that the best way to get over a deep hurt or offense is to keep it suppressed and unspoken. Nothing could be further from the truth. Darkness does not breathe good results. Jesus is in the Light. When you speak it out to God and consciously release it to Him, the light will expose it and you will be free.

Make a list of former exploiters, "haters", slave owners, those who share the ethnicity or culture of the offenders.

Don't forget to write down your brothers, relatives, friends and those of your own ethnicity who have offended you. Write down those who seem to have profited from slavery and the exploitation of the helpless. Put down anyone with whom you are angry or out of relationship with. Don't rush. Take your time.

**Step 6: Now is the time to systematically forgive each person and offense on that list. Go over this list one by one.**

After you have carefully and prayerfully completed your list, now is time to break free. Don't be alarmed or ashamed of the size of the list or of what is on the list. Keep a check on your emotions and focus on your relationship with God Almighty. He is bigger than any word on that paper.

Remember your job is to turn this case over to the judge (we do that through specific and deliberate prayer) and trust Him. Remember that you activate God's justice system when you forgive.

The Bible encourages us to speak out: with the heart man believes, but with the mouth confession is made unto righteousness. Don't rush through. Please don't say, "Lord, I forgive all these people" or "Lord, help me to forgive." or "Lord, I want to forgive 'so and so." Be specific. The Lord cannot do your work for you.

When you pray, make a clear choice and say it out loud so that your ears can hear the confession of your mouth: "Lord, I forgive (name/people) for (issue)" Keep going and cover every item on your list.

Here is a sample prayer that could serve as guide.

*Dear heavenly Father,*
*I thank you for your love, and kindness to me. I thank you for*
*accepting me as your Child and allowing me to be in your*
*presence right now. It is your kindness that has led me to*
*repentance. I thank you for your mercy also. I am asking your*
*grace and help as I take this step of forgiveness towards those who*
*have offended and hurt my ancestors and me. I have been hurt. You*
*know how I have been offended, and in obedience to your word*
*and because of your love in my heart I am ready to forgive them.*

(Get your list ready. Don't rush; The Lord is with you all the way).

*Lord, I forgive (use your list/name/people) for (issue).*

142

(Go through your list. When you have completed praying through your list, then continue by saying…)
*I release them and turn everything about it over into your hands.*
*I believe your Word and accept freedom from these offenses now and forevermore. They have no more control or power over me.*
*I thank you Lord for healing my emotions and memories.*
*I also ask you for wholeness of spirit, soul and body and for the restoration of your divine destiny*
*for all my descendants and for me. Through faith in Jesus Christ, I embrace the blessing of the Abrahamic covenant and the promises of your Word for myself and my household.*
*I thank you for hearing my prayers, healing my soul and setting me free from the past in the precious name of Jesus Christ My Savior, Redeemer and Lord. Amen.*

## Step 7: Stay for the healing! Verbalize your thankfulness and appreciation to God.

Sing a song of thanksgiving to Him. Take a minute to wait and allow the Holy Spirit to do a deeper work in your heart. No one shows up with a heart problem only to run out the door the moment the doctor starts the surgery. Let your soul bless the Lord. He is the Balm in Gilead. Just stay awhile in His presence.

## Step 8: This is the testimony stage.

This is the place of confessing with your mouth what God has down in your heart. Your testimony does something for you and for those who hear you.

Offenses carry generational consequences and scars. I encourage you to write a letter to your immediate family and share the steps which you have taken, and your reason for doing so. It is the right thing to do.

Don't rationalize anything. Base your action squarely on your willingness to obey Jesus' command to forgive those who have trespassed against you.

**Step 9: Keep a copy of the letter as a part of your legacy for the next generation.**

When the children of Israel came out of the Red Sea, they took up stones and left a memorial for all to see. The Lord instructed them to do this every time they experienced a great miracle so that when the future generations see the stones, they would be reminded of the great things the Lord did.

Your letter will help future generations to know that you and your family already settled these great offenses. This will save them from being exploited by the defeated devil and his puppets that preys on the suffering and hurts of people. Your letter will save them a lot of pain suffering and unsettledness and lift a huge burden from their shoulder. You will free them to properly honor and memorialize the great advances of those who died in the Atlantic triangle, labored in the cotton fields and the plantations by the success of their own lives. Your letter will serve to motivate others to also change the future and forgive.

# Chapter 10

## Expand Your Freedom

Follow up. Dedicate a special time of prayer, worship and meditation on God's Word for the next two months.

I encourage you to get with a mature Christians or your Church leaders for continued prayer. Take this time to focus on your continued healing and the renewal of your mind and outlook on life. Be sure to keep a close watch over your social media, entertainment choices and conversation. This includes TV, Internet, the songs your listen to, the books you read, and the people you listen to. Keep focus. Protect your freedom. Protect your thinking. Be vigilant. Practice quick forgiveness.

Here are some scriptures that will be helpful during your devotional time over the next 30 days:
1. Matthew 18:21-35
2. Matthew chapter 5
3. Proverbs 29:11
4. Mark 11:25
5. Jeremiah 29 20
6. Luke 17:3-4 21
7. Genesis 1:26-28
8. Acts 17:26-31
9. Genesis 9:9-19
10. Acts 10:28, 34-35
11. Proverbs 23
12. Romans 8:28-39 27.
13. John 9:28
14. Romans 12:14 -21
15. 1 Corinthians 4:12
16. Genesis 45:4-13
17. Matthew 6:1-15
18. Psalm 138

19. Matthew 4:1-11
20. Luke 6: 35-37
21. 1 Peter 1:18-19
22. Genesis 9: 5-6
23. Genesis 3:20
24. Malachi 2:10
25. Revelations 4
26. Psalm 68
27. Deuteronomy 8: 11-20
28. Matthew 28:18-20
29. Proverbs 24:17
30. Colossians 3:13

Here are some other topics that you could bring before the Lord during your 30 day follow up season of prayer and forgiveness. These issues are often associated with those who have been hurt or taken advantage of. Search the Bible to see what God says about these topics.

## 1. Freedom from rejection.

If you have feelings of unworthiness, abandonment, aloneness, disqualification or of being excluded, then express that to the Lord and look at scriptures that deal with your adoption as a Child of God. What is God's opinion of you? Whose report will you believe? Settle that question in prayer. Focus on building your personal confidence.

## 2. Freedom from the fear of men

Fear enters into our heart once we focus on the power and evil of men. However, this can be dealt with. Fear is described best in an acronym: F.E.A.R - False Evidence that Appears Real. The Bible says that "Perfect love casts out fear"(1 John 4:18). So acknowledge the fear, then accept God's love to erase it. He loves you too much to cause your fear to win. As the revelation of His love increases in your heart, fear will be cast out of your life. So shift your focus from people to God and accept that He is completely responsible for you, your future and your safety.

### 3.  Freedom from the fear of success.

If you have been hit on the head a few times or ridiculed a few times or encouraged to fail, then the idea of succeeding can be a hard thing to swallow. The fear of losing what you have will cause us to question whether or not you need to go through the trouble to get anything else. Have you ever been to the carnival and seen the pop up games? There is a big rubber hammer that you use to pound each toy that pops up. The fear of attracting "haters" and "the man" causes many to settle for less and keep their heads down. Who wants to be hit? Beware of the soft-bigotry of low expectation.

Verbalize your commitment to be "more than a conqueror through Christ." Pray and meditate on the Word of God that says you can do all things through Christ who loves you and gave himself for you (Philippians 4:13). Go ahead and say out loud; "In the Name of Jesus, I will succeed. I will fulfill my destiny.

### 4.  Freedom from the fear of failure.

Is your personal value tied to your success? One of the reasons why being disrespected often feels like a mortal wound, is that we have allowed the opinion of others to impact us deeper than God's view of us. Consequently the very thought of failing, "looking bad" or being disrespected is crushing. George Washington failed many times before being elected President. Call out your fears with a heart of faith in God's unconditional love for you.

## 5.  Freedom from manipulation and control.

A slick player knows how to exploit the weakness of the other side. The enemy of our soul does the same. Many are prospering and advancing themselves by exploiting the hurts of others today. When we are hurt, afraid and "not healed" people with selfish motives can use that wound to manipulate and control our votes, our money and our lives. Pray like Solomon did for wisdom, knowledge and understanding. Add discerning of spirit to that list of prayer needs.

## 6.  Freedom from visions of grandeur (self-exaltation).

We often develop sophisticated ways to protect ourselves when we have suffered deep putdowns, embarrassment or hurt. Often boasting, vision of grandeur, big and expensive lifestyles and excessive pride is the result. We feel the need to prove ourselves and present ourselves always in the best possible light. In other words there is a drive to campaign for recognition from everyone we come in contact with.

In prayer embrace the path of humility. Acknowledge that the primary person that you need to impress is Jehovah God. He is impressed with a broken and a contrite heart. He resists the proud, but gives grace to the humble. Read Romans chapter 12 and present yourself to the Lord - body, soul and spirit.

## 7.  Freedom from a poverty and dependency mentality.

It is important to address this issue during this season of healing, because over the years the true picture of God's plan for your prosperity have been marred. The history of slavery developed a dependency system that can now hurt you a lot more than it can help you. It will affect your political outlook on life. A result of the new life of forgiveness is the revelation that God is your source. Neither man nor government can ever give you what you are truly worth.

There may even be very well meaning programs that you have used and have helped you in the past that you must now re-examine. Ask yourself why do I need this? Is it truly helping me in the long run? For example, in the US, thousands of people lost their homes and ruined their credit, because at one time the government thought that they had a right to own a home. They did not care whether or not they were prepared to purchase one. Someone's good intention caused a lot of long-term damage. Pray now about the kind of financial future God has for you and your children.

### 8. Freedom from hunger for power, based on insecurity.

Power is intoxicating. The Bible warns about the terror of a servant who becomes King and of a mistress when she becomes the head of the house. The principle here is that unless a person is healed and walks in forgiveness, then power, authority or leadership become a means to exact revenge instead of serving the people.

Without a sense of having your future secured in Christ, we all will be tempted to use power improperly. Pray against this. Everyone cannot lead at the same time. However, don't run away from taking responsibility or positions of leadership. If you are a leader or have influence, then steward it well. Lead. Ask the Lord to use you for His glory. Love God. Love all the people. Serve the people, all the people.

### 9. Freedom from "the crab mentality" (jealousy of the success of others).

The "crab mentality" is the attitude that exists when opportunities are scarce, and when we focus on what man can give us instead of our destiny in Christ. It also comes as a result of thinking that we only get 1 slice of the "pie." If you put crabs in a bucket they will keep each other down, instead of working together to get everyone out. This happens when we view man as our source and our success is based on whether or not "they like us."

God commands us to love one another - seek their highest good ahead of our own. Commit yourself to live this kind of life and seek God's grace and help to do so. Ask the Lord to search your heart and prepare you to be a blessing to others. Help others succeed. There is room for you to also succeed.

## 10. **Freedom from sexual bondage.**

God certainly gave mankind the blessing of intimacy between a man and woman. Unfortunately, this beautiful communion is often abused. Sex is used to "heal" pains, to comfort or add value. Many times an individual's value is determined by their sexual appeal. Sex is used to project power, as a transaction and control. For many tormented by un-forgiveness, sex becomes a desperate attempt to escape from the mental torment. The result is that sex is used like cocaine, marijuana, alcohol, etc. Excessive and improper use is a sign of addiction and bondage.

Search the scripture for God's purpose for sex and commit yourself to sexual intimacy only with His blessing. When you are healed of un-forgiveness, you will have an increased capacity to love and to receive love from others. You will experience a whole new level of sexual intimacy when you walk in forgiveness. Remember, forgiveness frees you from the harassment of the tormentor. Prayerfully commit this area of your life to the Lord. Affirm that sex is not a method for "healing yourself" but that it is a part of your communion of love in a Godly marriage union.

## The Love Confession

Because I walk in the Love of God
I endure long and I am patient and kind.
I am never envious nor do I boil over with jealousy.
I am not boastful nor vainglorious, and
I do not display myself haughtily

The Love of God in me is NOT conceited, arrogant or
Inflated with pride. It is not impolite, unmannerly and
Does not act unbecomingly. God's love in me
Does not insist on its own rights or its own way. It is not
Self-seeking, touchy, fretful, nor resentful.
It takes no account of a suffered wrong.

Because I walk in that Love
I do not rejoice at injustice and unrighteousness, but
I rejoice when right and truth prevail,
I bear up under anything and everything that comes,
I am ever ready to believe the best of every person.

My hopes are fadeless under all circumstances, and
I endure everything without weakening, God's love
In me never fails, never fades out, never becomes obsolete or
comes to an end.

Because I walk in the Love of God, I also will never fail, and I will
never come to an end. Amen.

(This scriptural confession was adapted from 1 Corinthians 13:1-8 AMP
by Pastor Phillip Gordon of Lighthouse of Faith Ministries International,
Montego Bay, Jamaica.)

## Chapter 11

## Embrace Your Future

Forgiving others empowers you to pursue your destiny without fear. You are now ready to fight your own battles, to bear your own pains, to learn from your own mistakes, to celebrate your own victories, benefits from your successes and to give help to others in need. IF THE SON SETS YOU FREE, YOU ARE FREE INDEED (John 8:36). Walk in it.

Go and sin no more. Make the commitment to never again harbor un-forgiveness in your heart for anyone for anything. They aren't worth it. This freedom is for you and your household, both now and generations to come. You have now laid a new foundation for your descendants by forgiving and moving on to your destiny. Go for it!

It is important that from henceforth you think of yourself not as an ex-slave, descendant of slaves, a minority or a "recovering victim." You have a name. You have a destiny. You are unique. You have a nationality. Where we your born? Well, that is your nationality. Accept it, celebrate it, use it and move forward. In fact, you're even free to change your citizenship if you want to. Just be a good citizen where ever you go.

Your future is in the future! No baggage needed. No labels necessary. You are free. God heals and restores completely. Why should you limit the possibilities of your future to the horrors of the past? You are a child of the Most High God and everything He has belongs to you.

Take a few minutes and write down the things that you would like to do over the next five year. Go ahead and dream big. This is called your PERSONAL GOALS. Ask yourself, why are these things important to me? That is your PERSONAL VISION STATEMENT. It is a statement about where you see yourself in the future. It answers the question; why am I here?

Decide on what you can do right now as a first step towards your goal? Then begin. It doesn't matter how small the first step may be. Just start! Take a first step. There is no limit.

Place your personal vision statement on the mirror of your bathroom or someplace where you will see it every day. Pray about your goals every day.

Jeremiah 29 verse 11 is God's promise to you:
For I know the thoughts that I think toward you, says the Lord, thoughts of peace and not of evil, to give you a future and a hope."

The Today's English Version says; "I alone know the plans I have for you, plans to bring you prosperity and not disaster, plans to bring about the future you hope for."

New Century Version says; "I say this because I know what I am planning for you," says the Lord. "I have good plans for you, not plans to hurt you. I will give you hope and a good future."

World English Bible says; "For I know the thoughts that I think toward you, says Yahweh, thoughts of peace, and not of evil, to give you hope in your latter end"

We have the example of Israel to show that it can be done. They rose up out of hurt, slavery, violence and exploitation to fulfill their dream. You can too. It is not always easy. Not everyone will celebrate your life, but those who are important to you will. There will be new challenges, because many will not celebrate your new found freedom, but the benefits out way the risk.

Israel started prospering right there in Babylon, but it took 70 more years before Jeremiah's prophesy was completely fulfilled. They believed and practiced the promise. The Bible says, "Trust in the Lord with all your heart and lean not to your own understanding. In all your ways acknowledge him and he will direct they path" (Proverbs 3:5).

It is a reminder that those who trust in the Lord will never be ashamed. Delight yourself in the Lord and you will receive the desires of your heart. We are testimonies to the fact that the righteous will never be forsaken neither shall their descendants beg for bread.

You have a choice. You could keep your present perspective and continue to kick the can full of unsettled issues into your future and over to your descendants. They will have to be dealt with it at some time. The Bible says that if the fathers suck on sour grapes the children's teeth will be set on edge (Ezekiel 18:2). Our children will feel it, and they will feel it worse than we did. You could ignore these words and listen to the many voices who consider the way of forgiveness as simplistic or naive. Rev. Dr. Martin Luther King Jr. did not think forgiveness was simplistic nor naïve. He expected it, and so does Jehovah God. I agree with them. Do you?

The fact is that you will have to weigh the opinions and views of historians, commentators, singers, political leaders, professors, preachers, family historians and all human being against the Word of God. I encourage you to choose to walk in forgiveness. It's time. It's the best path forward.

Embracing the future requires steps of faith. It requires embracing the following perspectives:

**1. The Bible offers the only credible answer to the questions of life.**

The Bible teaches that God loves everybody. It teaches that all men are created equal. It teaches that success is for everyone. The problem is not the Bible. Your enemy is revealed by the Bible, Your enemy is the defeated devil and his subtle manipulations of humans' hearts. The Bible holds the key to LIFE in this new millennium. It is still credible and very relevant.

As you study the history of humanity you will see that Christianity has been a source for much LIGHT and LIBERTY to people all over the world. Even when the cross was used by wicked men and women to subjugate others, and to justify attitudes of superiority, racism, and prejudice, these actions were never, ever, justified, supported nor sustained by the Bible. Those who used the Bible and the name of Christ, to get public support for the evil intentions of their heart, did so on their own. They did not get those ideas from the Bible. They brought them to church with them. They got it from their culture, families, their selfish hearts and pride. Their teacher was not the Rabbi from Nazareth.

The slave masters saw the Bible as subversive and dangerous. In fact, many missionaries from the nation of Moravia left the heart of Europe, some even became slaves themselves in the West Indies, to teach the gospel and give hope to the slaves. The work of the Baptist Church and other Christian missionaries in championing the development of the poor stands in a class all by themselves. Illiteracy was and still is an effective method of control, worldwide. It was the availability of the Bible that triggered the reformation movement of the 1400s, and the global education movements.

The reformation made the Bible available to the common people, and consequently, learning is seen as a basic human right all over the world. The Bible liberates people. The Bible teaches that God loves everybody. There are no caste systems, no class system with God and no bad karmas. The Bible teaches of a community where everyone is treated equally under God. A kingdom where everyone has a good destiny. No one is a mistake or extra baggage.

All human beings have the same father, the same beginning, and the same end. This truth applies to the Roman soldier and to the Jewish prisoner in ancient Rome. It speaks to the "upper class" and the "lower class" of today in the same straightforward way. It speaks to descendants of slave masters and descendants of slaves, equally. There is simply no other Book like the Bible. It should not be taken lightly.

## 2. Life on earth was intended to be lived the way God intended: under His Kingship.

As Moses approached the last days of his life, he gathered the children of Israel together and instructed them to set their hearts on the Word of God. They were instructed to carefully teach their children these truths. He said to them, "It is not a futile thing for you, because it is your life, and by this word you will prolong your days in the land which you cross over to possess" (Deuteronomy 32:47).

This is very important. It affects the very quality of life that you will live. The Bible clearly tells us;

> It is written, Man shall not live by bread alone,
> but by every word of God. (Luke 4:4)

> It is not by might nor by power,
> but by my Spirit," says the Lord" (Zechariah 4:6).

> I beseech you therefore, brethren, by the mercies of God, that you present your bodies a living sacrifice, holy, acceptable to God, which is your spiritual service.
> And be not fashioned according to this world: but be ye transformed by the renewing of your mind, and ye may prove what is the good, acceptable and perfect will of God.
> (Romans 12: 1-3).

It is impossible to experience the promises of God without being reconciled to God. There will be no peace without the Prince of Peace. Consequently, peace will be absent from the city until the hearts of the people in the city are healed and filled with peace. Then and only then will we see peace! But it is possible.

Peace between the races or opposing groups cannot be legislated. Only people of different races and cultures who have experienced peace can then be catalysts for true peace. <u>And that is possible.</u> Others may give peace a chance for a time or as much as it benefits them. Christ releases us to give peace even when it hurts. But that's temporary, because justice will be served.

Blessed are the peacemakers for they shall be called the children of God (Matthew 5: 9).

## 3. We don't need another deliverer.

It's common for people to use the experience of the people of Israel as a road map for their own struggles. However, one must be very careful with this approach. For example, after Jamaica's independence in 1962, it was very popular for one party to crown their leader "Moses" while the other crowned theirs "Joshua." Often the development of the Nation was compared to the journey of Israel across the Red Sea into the Promise Land. I have always wondered: Why is it that the people are always crossing the Red Sea and never entering into the land? The journey of Israel is not completely applicable to the journey of people from Africa. We can learn some lessons from Israel, but there is no need to force fit the analogy.

We have been delivered already. Slavery is over. We don't need deliverers; we need prophets, priest and kings. We need Bible believing, Christ honoring and Holy Spirit empowered leaders. Prophets will hear the present and future word of God that edifies and gives direction to the people. The priests will minister to God for the people and be healers of breaches and wounds. Kings are leaders who lead into the possession of new territories and the carrying out of the Lord's directives. In the New Covenant era in which we live God has given leaders to the nation and apostle, prophet, pastor, teacher, and evangelist to the Church so that His will might be done on earth. We have leaders, but Jesus is our

157

Deliverer. He is the Messiah. He is our King. He is the King of Kings and Lord of Lords. We don't need another king. If your nation has a King, Queen or Queen's representative, and you want to keep that, fine, as long as they realize that Christ is King of kings, and they serve in that ceremonial role to serve the people. Christ is King all over the world.

We should make sure that we are listening to the instruction and wisdom that God has for us about life today. We need to grasp the NOW word of God. The Bible is relevant. The methods may change and strategies may vary, but the message never changes.

*God, who at various times and in various ways spoke in time past to the fathers by the prophets, has in these last days spoken to us by His Son, whom He has appointed heir of all things, through whom also He made the worlds; who ...when He had by himself purged our sins, sat down at the right hand of the Majesty on high having, become so much better than angels, as He has by inheritance obtained a more excellent name than they* (Hebrews 1: 1-2).

So according to Hebrews 2: 3 " ... we see Jesus, who was made a little lower than the angels for the suffering of death crowned with glory and honor, that He, by the grace of God, might taste death for everyone."

The Lordship of Jesus Christ has spiritual, political, social, and economic implications. He is God's final answer. He is relevant to your life. Christianity impacts public life. There is no separation between the Church and the State for Christians. Jesus Christ is Lord of All. We should not ignore His teachings on legislation, building the nation, commerce, building relationships nor His instruction to forgive. Once we ignore truth we are literally building our lives on sand. Jesus Christ is the foundational rock for all solutions.

## 4. No need to compare ourselves with Israel to gain a sense of legitimacy or acceptance.

There is no longer any need for spurious stories about the identity of the lost tribe of Israel. No need for long debates about the true descendants of Solomon and the Queen of Sheba. We don't have to try to connect with Israel to find our identity or significance. No need to be a Hebrew Israelite or claim Black Jewish. There is nothing wrong with being black and Jewish, if that is your actual birth ancestry. I'll call you whatever you want me to. There is just no need to claim those ceremonial titles to bring healing to our past. That does not work.

God's dealing with the children of Israel is not over, but it is not exclusive. An Israeli must submit to the kingship of God through faith in Jesus as the Messiah, just like all other human beings. God has a special plan for them, not because of their color, race or their nationality, but in spite of it. God has a plan to help them accept Jesus so that they will not perish. His agenda from the beginning was to bless all the families of the earth through Israel. In Genesis 12:1-3 the Lord told Abram:

> Get out of your country, From your family And from your father's house, To a land that I will show you. I will make you a great nation; I will bless you And make your name great; And you shall be a blessing. I will bless those who bless you, And I will curse him who curses you; And in you all the families of the earth shall be blessed.

God's plan is to bless you, even if you do not have one ounce of Jewish blood in you. Likewise all the promises of the abundant life are not automatic for any ethnic group, any nation, or any tongues. The Bible does not support the concepts of automatic blessing or cursing of any ethnic group. Notice that Abram's blessing was because he had faith in God and obeyed God, not in his ethnicity. The blessing was because of His faith.

Anyone can exercise this same faith of Abraham and connect to the Abraham covenant. That is the uniqueness of Israel, they still represent the promise of God to all mankind. They are a missionary nation, because of their ancestor's faith and obedience. The Church honors, loves and cares about Israel. But the blessing is not automatic. It's not in their skin. It's not in their blood, their brain, their cultural practices nor their DNA. It is in their faith and obedience.

For what does the Scripture say? 'Abraham believed God, and it was accounted to him for righteousness.' (Romans 4:3) Jesus made this clear to Nicodemus, the devout Teacher of the Jews; *Unless a man be born of the water and of the spirit He cannot enter the Kingdom of God. That which is born of the flesh is flesh and that which is born of the Spirit is spirit* (John 3: 5-6).

Peter received a vision from God, challenging his exclusive Jewish cultural paradigm. The Jews called certain people and things unclean, but Peter was asked, *"Why call what I have cleansed unclean?"* (Acts 10:18)

Simply identifying with Israel, simply quoting the scriptures, simply singing inspirational songs is not enough. The promise of Abraham and the promise of Jeremiah is only applicable for those who believe and respond in faith to the Gospel of Jesus Christ. And anybody, anywhere in any cultural can do that.

**5. Your history, regardless of the difficulties involved, does not automatically qualify you for a special victim status. God is just.**

I've come to appreciate the fact that people of all background go through problems in life. Economical, educational or social status does not preclude anyone from pain and suffering. How would you feel if the dress you worked so hard to buy for your daughter was left hanging in the closet, while she cries to go shopping? You would certainly do everything you can to help her to appreciate what she possesses. Likewise many of our answers are already within our reach.

The Bible informs us of an amazing piece of information: God has given to everyone the faith they need to start pleasing Him. He has given all human being what we need to live a blessed life. He gave us the innate ability to have faith in Him and to start now, in any circumstance.

*For I say, through the grace given to me, to everyone who is among you, not to think of himself more highly than he ought to think, but to think soberly, <u>as God has dealt to each one a measure of faith</u>. (Romans 12:3).*

"Pleasing God" is more than blind obedience. It means a willingness to RECEIVE FROM GOD. God is pleased when we expect to receive the answers to the prayers we have prayed. He is pleased when we acknowledge the provision, victories and breakthrough that He has given to us.

This scripture used to rub me the wrong way: *"For he that hath, to him shall be given: and he that hath not, from him shall be taken away even that which he hath"* (Mark 4:25).

I assumed that this scripture justified greed and hoarding and crony capitalism. I've since learned that this is a core principle to receiving and growing. If you refuse to use what you have, and to access what you have been given access to, you will lose it. To him who has what? Faith. To him who does not use his faith in Christ in dealing with living on earth, *"from him shall be taken away even that which he hath."* We lose faith in God when we refuse to exercise faith in God. Don't lose what truly belongs to you or what is currently accessible to you because of lack of obedience.

What is faith? It is hearing God's perspective on a particular issue, believing it, and making clear decisions based on that conviction. Faith is exercised when it is used. Faith grows when it is exercised. The physical, emotional, financial, and spiritual needs of your life are already provided for in Christ Jesus. There are creative answers to your situation. These answers are then channeled into all areas of your life as you activate your faith about your need. That's when we say, "The word becomes flesh." I like it when the word becomes flesh, don't you? That is when we actually get to experience the things we're hoping for.

I heard a great definition of faith recently that I must pass on to you. Faith is "trust in _____." You fill in the blank. Faith is not blindly following, because you have nothing to stand on. Faith is not wishful thinking. Faith is not spiritual roulette. Faith is not acquiescing to fate.

Some say, "Well, I guess I just have to have faith," meaning that we have decided to leave it up to chance or whatever the "Bigger Boss" decides. If you meant the God of the Bible by the "Bigger Boss" I want to assure you that His decisions are clear in the Bible and through the life and testimony of Christ Jesus. You don't have to guess. And He is your Father, not your boss!

You can take the next step with confidence and trust in the word and credibility of God. He never lies. You must know God's word or His perspective before you can walk in faith. Romans 10:10 says, *"Faith comes by hearing, and hearing the Word of God."*

## 6. The weapons of your warfare are not carnal.

Your spiritual perspective must now influence your worldview. It must now influence your voting. It must now influence your community structure and family expectation. There is a Biblical way of dealing with all things from finances to fiancées to government structure. You are free to ask the tough questions.

You are free to deal with topics that have been off limits for years: What is the current struggle for? Is it for national supremacy? Is it for racial or ethnic domination? Is it to settle racial, ethnic or national scores? Is it repatriation to Africa? Is it reparations? How does your Biblical worldview differ from the secular worldview on these same topics?

The question of your identity must also be settled. Who are you? Are you a Caribbean Christian, African- American Christian or a Christian first and then your ethnicity after? Are an African or are you a West Indian? Are you American or Russian or African or South African or Jamaican? Who are you? I say, pick the nation where you were born and embrace it. God allowed you to be born in that nation for a reason. If He wanted you to be Russian-American he would cause you to be born on the border between Alaska and Russia. Embrace and honor the country of your birth. But you can still honor and respect your roots. But identify with one at a time.

Some say, "Well, we were brought here against your will." Your fore parents were, but you weren't. Our fore parents had sex and that is why we are here. That is okay. I don't know if you had a choice in if and when and where you would be born, but I didn't. So take it up with God, and your parents, because you could have been born in Scandinavia or Jamaica or American. You could have been born to any set of parents in the world. You were not brought here on a ship. You were sent here by God. You are part of the answer. Welcome!

If you migrated to another country, and become a citizen of that country, then you made a second choice. That is also okay. It is now as if you were born in that country. Embrace it. Be one of them or don't live there. Why should you change the country you go to look like the one you left? They are two different places, two different cultures and two different people, and that is okay. Nobody is better than anybody, even if the economies are different. God is the same. He is a just God and His plans for you will work right where He places you.

I believe that as new creation in Christ the old must serve the new. Therefore, the Christian's first commitment will be as a citizen of the Kingdom of God and Christian principles and then to your earthly connections.

You must decide. You need to have a clear vision of the future that you are living for. You must have a clear sense of connection to the place where you are living and working right now. Regardless of your racial or national background, once you are "born again," you have placed your trust for life now and eternally into the hand of God through faith in Jesus Christ. You became a Christian first and everything else second.

Nero was mad that Christians would not say that Caesar was Lord. Nebuchadnezzar threw his most faithful servants into the fiery furnace because they would not dance to his tune and bow to his image. He later acknowledged that there was a God who made the heaven and who ruled in the dominion of men.

True Christianity does not disregard, erase nor forget nationality, race nor ethnic background. Nationality, ethnicity and racial issues are simply not the focus of a Christian's life and energy. Issues and people are not evaluated based on the color of their skins, their class or their history, but by God's principles. Christians put the contents of a person's character above their family line, skin color, education, money or any other visible signals. Christ first and all others after.

You are more than your roots. You need your roots. God gave them to us; they give us very valuable substance and anchoring in this big world. They give us a sense of identity and personality. However, a root cannot bear fruit. A tree cannot develop into its full potential by remaining in its roots. You need your roots, but you also need to grow up and out of the confinement of your roots into your divine destiny.

For Christians the primary warfare is fighting to be a true ambassador of reconciliation. Our task is first vertical and then horizontal - with God first and then with man. This is a spiritual movement not a social experiment. If you have not been "defeated by God" you will never win in life. Our orders are clear in the

Great Commission. We must reconcile men to God, their Creator. This is done through using whatever means possible to communicate God's love for people and His desire to patch up the differences between them. He wants to bless mankind. He wants to help people fulfill their destiny.

We are also called to reconcile men with each other. As Christians we bring healing and justice to incidents of exploitation, racism, violence, crime and look to Adam's fall and Cain's jealousy as the root of the system of evil in the world. We realize that, *"all have sinned and fall short of the glory of God"* (Romans 3:23). We understand now that *"there is none righteous, no not one"* (Romans 3:10). We are not short-sighted. We don't have amnesia and we do not have our head in the sand. We are well aware of what has happened, and what is happening. However, we believe that we have found the solution in the way of Christ. We believe that we can change the future by practicing forgiveness.

Therefore, in regards to the question of slavery or any issue of exploitation, we are not surprised by the actions of men, because we know that the hearts of men are wicked. We will not remain hurt by the rejections and wounds of people, because we understand that the source of that rejection is the defeated devil. He is no longer the one that our soul admires. We are no longer longing for approval, permission, validation or love from some "massa." We are healed and we are free. We also understand that not everyone will appreciate our new found freedom, but that too is the price of freedom. We still want to stay free, thank you.

The commendation or "get up and go" for life must be from God. Once we are aware of the kind of warfare that we are in, then the proper weapons can be employed. We fight hard with the uncommon weapon of love from a pure heart.

**7. The greatest challenge for today is to settle these questions in your heart: Who is your teacher? Who's got your ears? Whose report will you believe?**

Everyone has a teacher. Who is your teacher? Who is your teacher's teacher? Who is influencing your favorite singer? Who is the teacher of your favorite politician? Who are the philosophers behind the policy platform of the political party which you support? We should never take our marching orders and response cues from well meaning, well financed, and well-educated leaders who are unwilling to follow Godly principles. No leader should expect to command an entire ethnic group to follow them in this day and age. Sharing similar roots, shade of skin, history or even earlier struggles does not automatically mean that everyone has the same philosophy, perspective or solutions. In today's era of multi-ethnic relationships it is counter –productive to be pigeonholed into being a leader to one color, or one ethnic group.

We should never give any person such influence over our life. I wholeheartedly agree that we should respect history and honor those who deserve to be honored. However, the requirement to honor is not a demand to give up one's thinking capacity nor one's individuality. It is okay to disagree with a National Hero or former teacher or Civil Rights icon. It is okay to disagree with the founder of your organization. It is okay to respect the person and not accept their solutions. That is called freedom.

It is better to trust in the Lord than to put confidence in princes - even if they are home grown! Saul was still king when Samuel anointed David to replace him. Would your respect for Saul hinder you from embracing David as the new king? Ultimate obedience only belongs to God. Christ alone is the flawless leader. All leaders should be tested, and their words fully analyzed by the Word of God. We should love, honor, protect and follow those who follow a Biblical worldview.

Remember that the purpose of freedom is to be free. The purpose of leadership is not to preserve the leaders' status and position. The purpose of leadership is to lead, to point and to direct the way and preserve freedom The peoples' job is to decide for themselves whether or not they will follow.

## 8. Beware of the cycle of destruction.

We are not too modern, too advanced, nor too educated to escape the devil's old traps. Whenever we stray away from giving reverence and honor to God in our culture, in our streets, education, in politics, and morality we become sitting ducks for the enemy of man. Rome was once invincible. Hitler tore through Europe. The Soviet Union was unstoppable. The annals of history is littered with those who wagged their bony fingers in defiance of a gracious God. They died. The things they loved and the causes they were so proud of are now all gone. Wickedness does not last. Yet God remains steadfast in His love and His resolve to be reconciled to their children.

## 9. Those who have tasted the goodness of God spiritually, politically, and economically should be at the forefront of promoting the principles of the Bible in the public square.

If the Bible lacked influential in public decisions, Rev. Dr. Martin Luther King, Jr.'s message would not have resonated in the conscience of the USA. The "I have A Dream" speech is basically scriptures. People of African heritage must return God to the public forum. People of African heritage must return God to the classrooms. We will be charged to rise up and declare the virtue of Christ to suffering man and a hurting world.

Like Simon (an African) who lifted the heavy cross from the back of Jesus as He stumbled on His way to Golgotha, people of African heritage will be called upon to defend the cross around the world in these last days. You have experienced His great blessing. You have personally seen what can happen to a people who put their trust in God. You are seeing what happens when we turn

167

away from Him. There are mission fields waiting for the free, healed, and whole men and women of African roots to bear witness of the Way of Christ.

In the early 1900s entire tribes had visions of visitors that looked different from them coming to tell them about the God of heaven. I believe those visions are still happening. They might be waiting on you.

According to missions' experts, 65-83% of the world is closed to traditional missionaries today. The world is open to the non-traditional missionary. Your pain, your struggle, your life will be a great testimony to someone somewhere in the world. Go for it. Tell the story of how the Lord brought healing to you and your family.

Nations may come and nations may go, but following God is constant. Regardless of the talk of globalization and travel across the earth, we still cannot go outside of the influence of God. He is tracking your movements right now. It takes one generation of obedience in order for Him to reverse centuries of pain and bondage. Are you up to it? You can literally change the future by forgiving those who caused you harm.

## _____Quotables_____

- Not everything that sound good is good.
- The most popular tune may not be the right note.
- Don't allow your pain to overcome your wisdom.
- Forgive and be willing to take the risk.
- Faith in God will help you to love the unlovable.
- You have faith: in God or in your fears.
- Babylon is rough, but not "rougher" than God.
- Your perspective will determine your future.
- Don't judge people by their skin or their heritage; use Godly standards.
- Your life is as limited as you want it to be.

- You will hold on to as much pain, as you are comfortable with.
- To grow you have to get out of the comfort zone.
- If someone gives you a lemon, make some lemonade. Make enough for you and your family and share some with others. Start your own business to sell your homemade lemonade, and you will prosper.
- It is okay to expect to prosper.
- PERCEPTION IS 90% OF THE BATTLE.

### THE INVITATION:

The following verse was painted behind the choir loft at the Church where I spent my young days – The Southaven Pentecostal City Mission Church in Yallahs, St. Thomas, Jamaica.

This beautiful invitation has been a guiding light to my soul and my ministry.

I've found rest for my soul, and I hope that you will too.

*"Come unto me, all ye that labor and are heavy laden, and I will give you rest. Take my yoke upon you, and learn of me; for I am meek and lowly in heart: and ye shall find rest unto your souls."*
Matthew 11:28-29

### THE PROMISE:

*"For I know the thoughts that I think toward you, says the Lord, thoughts of peace and not of evil, to give you a future and a hope."*
Jeremiah 29:11
###

## ABOUT THE AUTHOR

Peter Burnett was born in Kingston, Jamaica, but grew up with his mother and other extended family members in the neighboring parish of St. Thomas. His personal mission statement is to "spend his life helping broken people." He became a member of the Southaven Pentecostal city Mission Church in Poormans' Corner, St. Thomas, and felt the call to preach at the tender age of 9 years old. In 1981 the God reminded of his calling by giving him life again after a drowning incident at Bailey's Beach in St. Thomas, Jamaica.

Peter has been married to Betty (since 1987) and they have 4 young adult children. Their cross-cultural marriage is a reflection of the power of unity in the Kingdom of God (Peter is from Jamaica and Betty from Florida/New York).

Peter and Betty Burnett are both ordained ministers. The Burnetts have been serving together in various types of Christian ministry since 1987. Their ministry challenges the status quo and motivate others to fulfill their potential in Christ. They believe that salvation through faith in Christ Jesus plus Christ-Centered education is the path to freedom for everyone. They have also demonstrated that nationality, color, place of birth, family heritage or family drama are the final indicators of a person's destiny or potential. Their ministry extends across all ethnic and socio-economic backgrounds to people from Africa, USA, Canada, Europe as well as throughout the Caribbean.

Peter and Betty Burnett returned to Montego Bay, Jamaica in December 2016 to establish a Christ-Centered, Open Access, Multi-disciplined and Holy Spirit - Empowered University. The mission is to impact the Church and all areas of society through Christ-centered higher education.

## For more information contact:

1. Email: pburnettmedia@gmail.com
2. Peter Burnett Media on YouTube.com
3. PCIChurchonline Community
4. ECUJamaica.com – website for Emmanuel Caribbean University, Montego Bay, Jamaica
5. Facebook.com/peterburnett04

US based office:
Emmanuel Caribbean Fellowship,
P.O. Box 380148, Murdock, FL 33938

In Jamaica:
P.O. Box 6525, Little River Post Office,
Rosehall, St. James, Jamaica

(876) 953-8596
contactecu@gmail.com

###

77293571R00095

Made in the USA
Columbia, SC
30 September 2019